MW01205139

How I Reversed My Heart Disease

by

Ron Burt

ALFIE PUBLISHING
Corpus Christi, Texas

RECIPE FOR LIFE
How I Reversed My Heart Disease

by Ron Burt

Published by:

ALFIE PUBLISHING
4817 Eider Drive
Corpus Christi, TX 78413

Publisher's Cataloging in Publication
(Prepared by Quality Books Inc.)

Burt, Ron, 1931 or 2-
    Recipe for life : how I reversed my heart disease / Ron Burt.

    p. cm.
    Includes bibliographical references and index.
    Preassigned LCCN: 96-96471
    ISBN 0-9646147-9-0

    1. Heart--Diseases--Nutritional aspects. 2. Heart--Diseases--Patients--Biography. I. Title.

RC684.D5B87 1997   615.854
                               QB196-40384
Printed in the United States of America

10 9 8 7 6 5 4 3 2 1

3212 E. Hwy 30
Kearney, NE 68847
800-650-7888

CONTENTS

-CONTENTS-

CHAPTER SIX

NOTICE

The information in this book is not intended as a substitute for any treatment prescribed by your physician.

Although several brands are mentioned, no payment or favor was received by the author for that mention. The recommendations are solely the opinion of Ron and Joy Burt.

ACKNOWLEDGEMENT

I would like to acknowledge the expert help June Custer has given to this project.

DEDICATION

This book is dedicated to my lovely wife Joy. It was through her strong determination to extend my life that she put me on the road to recovery by changing our lifestyle, thereby, reversing my heart disease.

INTRODUCTION

This book details my own personal program how I reversed my heart disease. It can serve as a program for individuals who have loved ones they want to see grow old and enjoy an extended quality life - a desire to view a sunset or a sunrise and enjoy all of God's creations. If you do not start a healthy program for yourself, do it for your loved ones. Life means more than fatty unhealthy foods.

You may be committing suicide with your lifestyle and it could be just a matter of time before a degenerative disease consumes you. After all, cardiovascular disease is our number one killer. Yet, heart disease responds most readily to improvements in nutrition and lifestyle.

There is a great deal you can do concerning your health. A change of lifestyle, with a low-fat vegetarian diet and exercise program, could reverse your condition. However, most doctors will never mention reversing heart disease other than through medication and/or surgery. They are trained to prescribe drugs and perform surgery. Also, they assume that most people will never change their diet to a degree that will reverse a degenerative condition.

With a diet based on whole grains and vegetables in conjunction with daily exercise, nearly everyone can expect significant vascular renewal within a few weeks.

To get started, the only thing you need is to have a strong desire to live. It's your choice. Live to eat, or eat to live!

CHAPTER ONE - AT DEATH'S DOOR

Spring was in full bloom and the month of April brought all the beauty of the flowers and the singing of birds. The sound of a tennis racquet connecting with a tennis ball that echoes across the court is exhilarating to a tennis player. Forty-love - just one point to make for our tennis doubles team and the game was ours. The toss for the serve was perfect. A loud "pow" echoed across the court as the racquet struck the ball sending a strong delivery to my opponent's back hand. The ball was returned high and to the middle of the court allowing for an easy point. As I struck the ball, a strange pressure-like sensation emerged in my chest. This constant and uncomfortable pressure made me feel short of breath. After a few minutes, the pressure subsided and eventually ceased. I ignored it until the pain returned a few minutes later.

The activity that surrounds a tennis club after a match is exciting. Win or loose, you remember the good shots and enjoy discussing it with your tennis friends. Why should anyone be ill during a time such as this? As we sat talking and joking, the pressure I experienced began to haunt me. However, I didn't want to spoil the day but knew that I should tell my tennis partner, my wife Joy. After explaining the experience of the pressure in my chest, she insisted I see my doctor.

"It's probably your heart" explained the doctor. "We'll give you a treadmill test which should tell us something, and then we can go from there."

The treadmill test exhausted me. I fought for each breath of air as I laid on a small table recuperating. Now my cardiologist said,

"There is definitely a problem here. We'll schedule an angiogram which will show us exactly where and what arteries are blocked and how severe your case may be."

The angiogram revealed two blocked arteries that would require bypass surgery. This devastated me. How in the world could I be a heart patient in my present condition at the age of forty-nine? I have never smoked, have never been overweight and exercise regularly. In addition, I am a non-drinker and have never abused my body with drugs.

"You have not contributed to your condition and should not be here", the cardiologist commented. "However, your arteries are in bad shape and you must undergo bypass surgery. In fact, your condition is bad enough that you should have died on the tennis court!"

This was April 1981. After I was assigned to a room, coronary artery bypass surgery was scheduled. I counted ten different doctors that visited with me; the team of heart surgeons that would be performing the operation, the anesthesiologist, the cardiologist, etc.

"We have you scheduled for two bypasses," explained my doctor. "The procedure will be no greater for one bypass than for four bypasses. The risks and trauma of this operation are the same, so don't be alarmed if you require more than two. We will be in position to make as many as necessary and you will feel no better or worse on the number of grafts that are made."

A speedy recovery allowed me to be back on the tennis court eight weeks after surgery. My attitude prior to and after surgery was positive, and I was not going to allow surgery to stop my active lifestyle.

"Do exactly what you were doing prior to your surgery. It's okay to continue with the same diet you had before your bypass," the doctor commented.

Wrong!

I should have been more informed as to what caused my condition and what could be done to reverse a failing heart. My doctor was not aware of any alternate treatment other than modern medication and surgery, or at least he did not express his knowledge of other treatments. The year 1981 was not a banner year for low-fat diets.

My doctor attributed the blocked arteries to genetic heredity. True, my family had a history of heart disease. My dad died from cardiac arrest, and he had three cousins who died at the ages of thirty-eight, thirty-nine and forty-two, all within an eighteen-month period. Scientists have determined that some people inherit genetic predisposition to disease. Those with one or more relatives with a particular disease are more likely to develop that disease. In some disorders, the genetic component is so strong that nothing can be done through modern medicine and surgery to alter the course of the disease.

This was the position that my doctor took in regard to my case. Nothing could be done to alter my heart disease, and there was nothing to be done to correct it out side of using modern medicine and surgery.

I do not believe that my problem was solely from inherited genes. In 1981, this was my belief, but not now. Education has changed my thinking, and I now know that what you eat is the determining factor that controls heart disease whether you have a healthy heart or a failing one.

No change in my diet was made from 1981 to 1988. In May of 1988, severe angina reappeared in my chest. I was experiencing a lot of pain and would be facing yet another surgery - coronary angioplasty.

Coronary angioplasty was first introduced in September 1977. At the time of my bypass surgery in 1981, my cardiologist was not convinced that angioplasty was the proper procedure for me. He said he wanted to wait until angioplasty had proven itself in the medical field and regarded a minimum five-year study. His group of cardiologists were scheduled for a series of conferences and studies of coronary angioplasty in August of 1981, four months after my bypass surgery.

Now, in 1988, my cardiologist had almost seven years experience in angioplasty surgery and considered me a good candidate for the procedure known also as balloon angioplasty. It is technically known as Percutaneous Transluminal Coronary Angioplasty, or PTCA. This procedure was found to be capable of repairing (a temporary repair) the arteries of the heart. More than 150,000 procedures are performed each year in the United States.

Being a relatively simple procedure, a cardiac catheterization (same as for bypass surgery) is performed preceding angioplasty to locate blockages. When a blockage is located in a coronary artery, a small wire is advanced forward. A collapsed balloon wrapped around the wire is guided into the middle of the blockage. When positioned correctly, the balloon is inflated forcing the blockage to open. The artery is stretched and the cholesterol plaque is pulverized, thus opening the artery for a normal blood flow.

A ninety-five plus percent blockage (see illustration No. 1) was located during this latest heart cath. The first week of June 1988 I was given a balloon angioplasty.

After this surgery, a change of diet was still not part of my health program. Joy and I had given up tennis by 1984 and were on a walking program that satisfied our exercise needs. We walked in our neighborhood or at the local mall. Also, I walked on a treadmill at home when the weather did not permit walking outside.

My medication consisted of Cardizem, Pravacor (a cholesterol lowering drug), one aspirin daily and I wore a nitroglycerin patch. Prior to taking Pravacor, Mevacor was prescribed as my cholesterol lowering medication. Studies have shown that Mevacor (lovastatin) lowers the levels of coenzyme Q10 in the bloodstream, an antioxidant that helps the body resist heart damage. My cholesterol prior to my 1981 surgery was 211.

Two years later, after the 1988 angioplasty surgery, I began experiencing pain in my chest again. In June of 1990 I underwent another cardiac catheterization. This test showed that the artery that was bypassed in 1981 was one hundred percent blocked. The saphenous venous segment used for the bypass showed a sixty percent blockage and the artery where the angioplasty was performed began to show a ten percent build-up of blockage. The crowning blow came when my doctor pointed out that there was another area of blockage forming in the LAD (left anterior descending) artery. This area could not be corrected with bypass surgery or with angioplasty.

CORONARY ARTERY DIAGRAM

NAME *R. Ant*

DATE *5/31/89*

DOCTOR *TED*

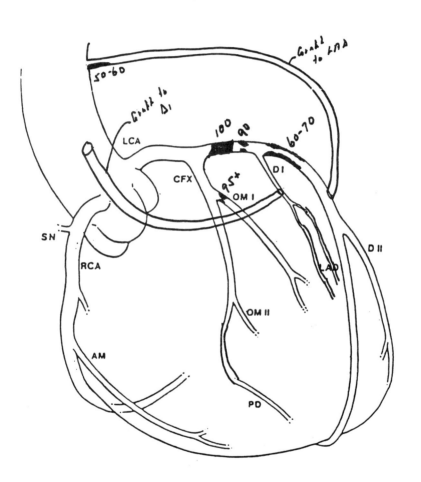

Illustration No. 1
Coronary Artery Diagram on May 31, 1988

Bypass grafts must be attached to the recipient artery downstream of the blockage. In my case, this was not technically possible because the artery had diffuse blockages throughout its entire length. (See illustration No. 2)

Now, and NOT before now, a change in diet became a factor in correcting my failing heart. My doctor told me that my years were numbered. A change in lifestyle must be made. In effect, I was dying of a failing heart. My doctor said that I should retire, but I pleaded with him to let me continue working.

At this point, Joy and I went on a low-fat diet. We ate only the white meat of chicken and turkey and controlled the amount of oily foods we consumed. Boy, we thought we were doing great! Big mistake. We were not even touching the tip of the ice-berg as far as a good healthy diet was concerned. We fell into the trap that so many people are in. We believed that we were eating a good healthy diet.

I continued with my work but cut back to four days a week and reduced my work day from eight hours to six. After one year, growing weaker as each month passed, in July 1991, my doctor declared me to be medically disabled due to significant coronary disease. In August 1991, my company placed me on long term disability and I retired.

Our walking program continued along with the diet that we started in June 1990. My physical activity was reduced considerably due to the lack of energy and just plain scared to death that any exertion would put too much strain on a weak heart causing a cardiac arrest.

Simple tasks, such as mowing the grass, were very difficult to perform. Even though I had a self-propelled

CORONARY ARTERY DIAGRAM

NAME *Rer Ben?*
DATE *6/13/90*
DOCTOR *JEO*

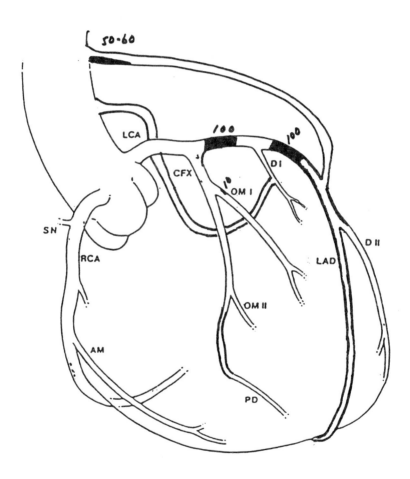

Illustration No. 2
Coronary Artery Diagram on June 13, 1990

lawn mower, periods of rest had to be taken after traversing the yard a couple of times.

I didn't have enough strength to mow both front and back yards the same day. Mowing the back yard was put off for another day. Carrying light brush and trash from the back yard to the front became burdensome which frustrated me.

Exercising became difficult. I could not walk more than fifty yards before experiencing pain in my chest, left arm and shoulder. At this point, I accepted the fact that my heart was not, and could not, get any better than it was. I felt I was on a downhill slide with no recovery in sight. In other words there wasn't much hope for me. My days were numbered. The luxury of growing old was not in my grasp.

CHAPTER TWO - ROAD TO RECOVERY

Other facts about heart bypass surgery strengthened my fears. After my surgery, I thought my heart was as good as new. This was not true. Other arteries showed some blockage but not enough to justify bypass surgery at this time. However, the blockages were there and would continue to increase over a period of time, and they, too, would require bypass surgery or angioplasty. Also, new blockages can appear in arteries that were normal at the time of an earlier surgery.

Atherosclerosis takes years to develop in the arteries of the heart. Such factors as many years of smoking, a high-fat diet, high blood pressure, diabetes and stress all contribute to the slow but progressive process of hardening of the arteries.

Surgery is **not** a permanent cure for heart disease. It is simply a stop gap - a temporary repair. Coronary disease accelerates after a bypass operation with new blockages developing as early as two years after the surgery. More than fifty percent of the arteries that have been bypassed will reveal new evidence of disease one year after the operation. Some bypass grafts can shut down with complete blockage. This was a post-operative condition which concerned me. How long would this repair job hold up?

Ten years after an operation, a high percentage of venous grafts show signs of trouble - between thirty to fifty percent will be totally blocked. About thirty percent will have developed significant narrowing, thereby limiting the flow of blood to the heart. Many patients will be faced with a second operation.

Coronary artery bypass surgery is often called an "overprescribed and unnecessary surgery" by many leading authorities.

If doctors have tried everything and nothing is working, that's when surgery is appropriate.

We patients should remember to be smart consumers. There are very few cardiac crises that require immediate angioplasty or surgery. With coronary artery disease, the narrowing in the arteries has been there a long time.

We need to be cautious about agreeing to invasive procedures. When your doctor says, "We must do emergency angioplasty or bypass surgery to save your heart," do not think that you have no position to argue, because you should argue. There is no evidence that bypass surgery is more effective than medical treatment in this situation. In fact, it may be more dangerous. What doctors rarely tell you is that the procedure for angioplasty subjects you to a radiation dose equal to ten thousand chest x-rays!

For years and years we have been caught up in a "passive patient syndrome" due to relying more and more on doctors and technology. Surgery is often an elective procedure rather than a mandatory one. Many doctors may feel obligated to operate because of accreditation requirements for hospitals.

If I only knew back in 1981 prior to my heart surgery what I know now, surgery would not have been an option. I would have gone on a low-fat vegetarian diet in a New York minute! Surgery is risky and causes much suffering and pain - it should not be step one. *Research about your condition and be informed*!

I had joined hundreds of thousands of heart patients in identical circumstances. It's sad that many in this elite group depend solely on the medical profession to cure their failing heart. A program to reverse heart disease by a change of lifestyle and getting back to natural unprocessed foods separated me from this group.

A determined and loving wife refused to believe that synthetic drugs were the only answer. She thoroughly believed there must be another way to cure heart disease rather than resorting to medication and/or surgery. In June of 1993, a ray of hope came. We just happened to tune into an interview on television featuring Dr. Dean Ornish. He was explaining his method of reversing heart disease without medication or surgery but with diet and exercise. We were fascinated by his theory. We knew this was the answer we had been searching for. The following day we visited a local book store and purchased a copy of *Dr. Dean Ornish's Program for Reversing Heart Disease.*

In July of 1993, Joy and I started an ultra low-fat vegetarian diet program. We went cold turkey (pardon the pun). No meat and only non-fat dairy products. We considered this to be an eatable life insurance.

We used the Dr. Dean Ornish program as a basis, however, we took it several steps beyond. In this book, it is our goal to outline the steps that we took to achieve this. It is a simple procedure, and, if followed, could reverse your heart disease.

Results will come almost immediately. I was noticing some change for the better within the first five weeks after I started my diet.

Six months into the diet program, I was able to cease taking the Pravacor and stopped wearing the nitro-patch.

These results made sense to me, just as it is in the case of smokers. Smokers who quit smoking will reduce their risks of having a heart attack to the same level as those who have never smoked at all. There is ample evidence that within just two years after quitting, ex-smokers will have cut their risks of having fatal heart attacks in half. The healing process begins immediately when a person stops smoking.

This is what the American Cancer Society says about smoking:

"As soon as you snuff out that last cigarette, your body will begin a series of physiological changes.

"Within twenty minutes: Blood pressure, body temperature and pulse rate will drop to normal.

"Within eight hours: Smoker's breath disappears. Carbon monoxide level in blood drops, and oxygen level rises to normal.

"Within twenty-four hours: Chance of heart attack decreases.

"Within forty-eight hours: Nerve endings start to regroup. Ability to taste and smell improves.

"Within three days: Breathing is easier.

"Within two to three months: Circulation improves. Walking becomes easier. Lung capacity increases up to thirty percent.

"Within one to nine months: Sinus congestion and shortness of breath decrease. Cilia that sweep debris from your lungs grows back. Energy increases.

"Within one year: Excess risk of coronary heart disease is half that of a person who smokes.

"Within two years: Heart attack risk drops to near normal.

"Within five years: Lung cancer death rate for average former pack-a-day smoker decreases by almost half. Stroke risk is reduced. Risk of mouth, throat and esophageal cancer is half that of a smoker.

"Within ten years: Lung cancer death rate is similar to that of a person who does not smoke. The pre-cancerous cells are replaced.

"Within fifteen years: Risk of coronary heart disease is the same as a person who has never smoked."

So, shouldn't your heart begin to heal when you stop poking fat into your arteries? The answer is YES! I am living proof. In July 1995 I ceased taking Cardizem (my doctor previously said I should take Cardizem for the remainder of my life!). My cholesterol is now 148, with *no* medication. I am completely free of all medication. I have reversed my heart disease, and you could too!

The body is self-healing, which we all have experienced when recovering from cuts, bruises, broken bones and various other injuries. For the body to reverse and cure degenerative diseases, it must be supplied with healthy, natural nutrients in order for the healing process to take place. Providing the body with appropriate molecules from nature will start the self-healing process.

Clean food, clean water and clean air, and the fifty essential factors they contain, are the natural sources of healing molecules.

It takes about two years for the body to rebuild itself completely. Done properly, this is also the time it takes to completely reverse a malnutrition or internal pollution-induced degenerative condition and to remove accumulated toxins from the body.

Fifteen months into our program I was able to climb a thirty-five foot cottonwood tree and cut it down with a chain saw, working at the top of the tree cutting branch by branch until only a two foot trunk was left. This laborious activity was evidence that our program was effective in reversing my heart disease. My energy had soared.

Eighteen months into our program I commenced work on a Spring garden. This required digging up all the carpet grass in a ten feet by ten feet area and spading up the ground about eight inches deep. It also required removal of several cottonwood tree roots that traversed the garden area. One, six inches in diameter, curved throughout the length of the area. After I cleared the surrounding dirt, the root had to be cut with an ax where it entered into the garden area and at the other end where it branched into two roots going under a concrete walk near the house. The portion of this root removed from the garden area was approximately fourteen feet in length. It was a real "garden monster!"

Twenty-eight months into the program I tackled a job that had been put off for several years due to my health. This was jacking-up my work shop (12' by 20') that had settled too close to the ground. I rented four twenty-ton hydraulic jacks to do the job. Four ditches, which were two feet deep and two square feet wide were dug. Roots from the same cottonwood tree were smack dab in the ditch areas and had to be removed just as they were in the garden area.

The jacks were placed in the ditches, and I proceeded to gradually jack the building up approximately eight to ten inches. After the building was at the desired height, I placed eight solid concrete blocks (8"x8"x16") strategically under the building. All of this work was done in a six hour period, and by myself.

Thirty-two months into the program I again took on another long overdue project - painting my home. Nearly all of the flashing boards on the eves had to be replaced. This was done and a little scraping was required in certain areas. Our home is two stories, therefore, this required many trips up and down the ladder to the upper story and eves of the house where half of the six gallons of paint was used to paint our home and work shop.

Thirty-four months into the program, and gaining strength each month, our closed-in patio was in need of much repair; demolition was due. This fourteen feet by twenty four feet area was coming down. I tore off the old roof and replaced it. We had three sliding glass patio doors (6'x6'-8") across the back section which I removed. Then, with crow-bar and hammer, I demolished the paneled walls, placing four (4"x4"x8') pillars to support the completed roof.

All of the roofing debris was cut up into small pieces with a skill saw and placed in plastic trash barrels and carried to the street. The material from the walls, and some fifty pound concrete blocks (four of them), were loaded in my pick-up and carried to the city dump. All of this work was done by me alone.

I am now into the fourth year of our healthy program, and my quality of life continues to improve.

A person doesn't need to be a rocket scientist to grasp the biological basis of health and healing. When you realize that health is inherent and that disease is a departure from health, the rest of the natural healing approach follows logically. We have gathered the details and have put together a natural healing program for you.

Joy has devoted many hours researching (over the last three years) the benefits that natural foods, herbs, vitamins and food supplements offer. This research has provided us with a natural healthy heart program that we can live with.

Our health program is not only about survival; it is about quality of life. Moderate dietary changes are not enough to reverse heart disease, however, if you choose to start in moderation, eat a little meat occasionally, and gradually reduce your meat to zero, this will be okay - not the ultimate program, but it will start you on a healthy diet.

In my case, we felt a sense of urgency, and being strong disciplinarians, we launched this program with no holds barred. We were determined to reverse my heart condition and have a better quality of life to boot.

No one knows when the body has been damaged beyond recovery, therefore, no one should be written off as hopeless.

It would be great if everyone would turn to a healthy diet and do something to prevent these degenerative diseases.

The price for choosing one's food according to the dictates of the palate will have to be paid for by chronic ill health and physical suffering.

You must set your priorities in order to reverse your heart disease. You need to be on a very low-fat vegetarian diet with an exercise program. Eating fat not only makes you fat but also gives you heart disease and creates other health problems as well. Each gram of fat contains nine calories, whereas, protein and carbohydrates have only four calories per gram.

On our low-fat vegetarian diet you do not count calories or fat grams. It's a pain and a bore and takes the fun out of eating. You can eat all you want and never go hungry.

We went on a vegetarian diet because of the fat content in all meat, including poultry and dairy products, except for non-fat and low-fat dairy products.

Cholesterol intake is not our prime concern. Even though we are very cognizant of cholesterol and control consumption, the ingredient that is more important to us, and what we try to eliminate, is fat. *Reduce as much fat as possible from your diet and eat an abundance of fresh vegetables and fruit. We believe this is the key to reversing heart disease.* Vegetables and fruits are antioxidant-rich, therefore, allows nature to work for us. They have not invented a pill that can do what nature does best.

I can hear it now; Well, what in the world are we going to eat? The answer is - plenty! You will see what I am talking about in the recipe section.

Most healthy adults need only three to six grams per day of EFA (essential fatty acids). This depends on your size and sex. One tablespoon of any oil or butter contains almost fourteen grams of fat. Fat does taste good, but as you decrease the amount of fat in your diet, your palate will begin to readjust. After awhile, you'll find that the food on a low-fat vegetarian diet tastes delicious. Eating unhealthy food will soon become repulsive to you.

Most doctors are trained in drug-oriented medical practices remain skeptical about natural approaches to health. Such doctors fail people like myself who struggle to improve health through natural means.

Doctors did not choose to ignore nutrition while in medical school. Lack of their nutritional education is attributed to the drug-oriented curriculum imposed on them by large pharmaceutical companies. Over the years they positioned themselves so they can and do have a strong influence over the course content of medical studies and the politics of medical associations.

Regardless of the poisonous effect to human health, synthetic drugs are patented to protect huge profits for drug companies that manufacture them. These patented drugs are used to suppress symptoms of disease. The body warns us when something is wrong by various symptoms and to suppress this warning with drugs will only cause our health to continue to deteriorate. This makes no sense at all. Synthetic drugs are likely to produce more free radicals in our body, doing further harm. When our diets become natural, free radicals cease to be a major concern.

We must not give up our responsibility for good health. Taking charge can be done with our knives, forks, spoons, cups and plates. We must think about what we put on them and in our mouths.

Causes of degenerative disease include nutrient deficiency, food pollution and imbalance. The food that our ancestors ate had the essential nutrients, but these nutrients have been removed from natural, whole foods by processing. Processing causes nutrient loss that occurs during storage and transporting and by imbalance farming methods that leave soils depleted.

Degenerative diseases, in fact, are almost always caused by malnutrition and/or internal pollution. These diseases can be reversed and cured only by nutrient enrichment and/or detoxification. Diet is the most important single factor for prevention of atherosclerosis.

Sixty-eight percent of the population dies from degenerative conditions, but less than 0.5 percent of degenerative conditions are caused by bad genes.

Effective treatment for these diseases requires a return to whole food habits followed by our ancestors, to food choices which adequately cover our known nutrient requirements and to a way of eating more in harmony with the ways of nature.

You cannot have long life and good health just by falling off a stump. We must learn to care for our own body. Since we are the only one living in it, we feed and direct it, and we alone bear the consequences of our eating habits and lifestyle.

With our program you can feel great, reverse your heart disease, lower high blood pressure, and help a multitude of problems including diabetes, arthritis and the prevention of colon cancer.

The "cure" for heart disease is quite basic - lifestyle and diet. You can literally eat your way out of heart disease, so let healthy food be your medicine!

When we examine the causes (bad nutrition, stress, etc.) of degenerative diseases, we can begin a program to reverse these conditions. What was it that caused you to be in this condition in the first place? God gave most of us a healthy body at birth. Between then and now we have knowingly, or unknowingly, abused it. What is very discouraging is the unknown things that we do to harm the body. One of the big 'unknowns' is what is in our food that destroys the body. Many of us never give it a second thought when we enter the supermarket, pick up a loaf of bread, grab a package of margarine, potato chips, etc., what we are about to put into our body.

Not any packaged products will indicate on the label that "hydrogenated oil" is bad for us and can cause degenerative diseases, such as we might have right now! This is why it is important that we must research these ingredients and understand what we are doing to our health and eliminate the unknown and be properly informed. By doing so, we cut our risk tremendously. Some of the topics that we should be aware of are listed in this chapter. Do not limit your knowledge to only these, but explore more topics concerning your health. We must choose between toxic and natural treatment, and we should not expect good results from combining them. We have to have a strictly nutritional program.

- CHOLESTEROL -

Much publicity has been devoted to cholesterol and its effect on the human body when the level is excessive. The mere thought of having a high cholesterol reading can terrify the minds of misinformed people. This form of terror is big business for doctors, laboratories and drug companies. It's a powerful marketing tool for vegetable oil and margarine manufacturers who advertise their products to be free of cholesterol.

We've been brainwashed about cholesterol and its relationship to heart disease. Like any skillful scam, the perpetrators took a shred of factual information and created a plausible, compelling scenario. Cholesterol levels are an important diagnostic tool - don't ignore them. However, cholesterol has been given far too much importance. There is much we don't understand about heart disease even though information about drugs and surgery is communicated to patients as if it were gospel.

Cholesterol is a hard, waxy, fat like substance. It is essential for our health but it is not necessary to obtain it from the food that we eat. For about seventy percent of the U.S. population, eating high cholesterol foods does not raise cholesterol. In most people, less than five percent of the cholesterol in the bloodstream gets there through diet. Your body manufactures about seventy-five percent of its cholesterol from the foods you eat. Generally, if your diet contains more cholesterol, your body responds by making less. In most people, excess cholesterol is broken down by the liver and excreted.

The body can acquire cholesterol from other materials when foods break down, such as, sugars, fats and proteins. This material is 2-carbon acetates. This takes place when the total intake of these foods supply the body with calories in excess of the body's requirement.

The more excess calories that are consumed, especially from products containing sugars and saturated and other non-essential fatty acids, the more pressure there is on our body to make cholesterol. Plus, the more stress we are under, the more cholesterol the body manufactures, because cholesterol is the precursor of stress hormones.

Cholesterol can come from foods or be manufactured in our body. Foods containing cholesterol come from animal sources such as eggs, meat, dairy products, fish and shellfish. About 250 mg of cholesterol is found in one egg, each 1/4 pound of butter and each 1/4 pound of liver but fish and shellfish contain less.

In the United States, the average adult will consume around 800 mg of cholesterol daily. About forty-five percent comes from eggs, thirty-five percent from meat and twenty percent from dairy products. Approximately half of the dietary cholesterol is absorbed, and the rest passes through our digestive systems unused.

A unique aspect of cholesterol is that the body can make it, however, once it has been manufactured, the body cannot break it down. On the other hand, sugars, fatty acids, amino acids and nucleic acids can all be separated and turned into carbon dioxide, water and ammonia. This means that cholesterol must, and can only, be removed from the body through the stool in the form of bile acid and cholesterol molecules.

Dietary fiber increases the removal of cholesterol. The absence of fiber will cause ninety-four percent of the cholesterol and bile acids to be reabsorbed and recycled. Due to this, low-fiber diets will increase blood cholesterol levels.

Approximately two-thirds of U.S., European and affluent populations world-wide suffer from atherosclerotic deposits to a degree. Arteries are narrowed by deposits made of proteins, fats, cholesterol and minerals. This narrowing of the arteries causes the flow of blood to slow down. Plus, saturated or denatured fatty acids and cholesterol make the platelets sticky, therefore, increasing the risk of a clot forming. A combination of atherosclerosis and clots can completely block an artery, cutting off oxygen and nutrients to the cells of the part of the body supplied by that artery, causing the death of those cells.

Strokes occur if an artery to the brain is blocked. The severity of the stroke is determined by the size and location of the blocked artery. The stroke could be minimal, or it could be fatal. Angina, chest pain, is caused when stress or exertion is placed on narrowed arteries leading to the heart or after a meal high in fat which makes the blood thicker and less capable of supplying oxygen. A heart attack results when arteries supplying the heart are blocked, and if a clot blocks an artery in the lungs, pulmonary embolism occurs. Impaired circulation caused by blocked arteries to the legs may lead to gangrene. When arteries supplying sense organs are blocked, deafness and blindness may occur.

Arteries are hardened by atherosclerotic deposits. This causes the blood pressure to rise because of the arteries' resilience which normally takes up the pressure generated by heartbeats is lost. Further damage results because a heavier load on the heart and kidneys, when prolonged, leads to water retention and heart and kidney failure.

To say high cholesterol causes heart disease is like saying a high fever causes a cold. High cholesterol is a symptom of heart disease, but there is no evidence that it causes heart disease. It may be more accurate to say that heart disease causes high cholesterol. It is believed that high cholesterol is a symptom of an underlying nutritional deficiency or it is the body's response to damage by rancid fats. The accumulation of cholesterol and other fats on the blood vessels represents the body's attempt to repair the damage. Folks who control their cholesterol intake through diet do tend to suffer from less heart disease, but this has more to do with the lifestyle changes involved in lowering cholesterol.

Nutritional programs for cholesterol reduction do more than just decrease cholesterol; they also improve cardiovascular health. Excess body fat increases blood cholesterol and triglyceride levels. Losing weight lowers both cholesterol and triglyceride levels.

Refined sugars and starches (such as white flour, white rice and pasta), and refined or altered fats and oils raise cholesterol levels. A return to natural, complex, high fiber carbohydrates and natural, unrefined fats and oils lowers cholesterol. Removing refined (especially sugar-containing) foods from our menu is surprisingly effective in lowering cholesterol and triglycerides.

Smoking and stress raises cholesterol levels and so does coffee, tea and colas.

The more saturated fat you eat, the greater your risk of coronary heart disease even if your blood cholesterol level and blood pressure do not rise very much.

The two leading causes of death among affluent people are strokes and heart attacks. World wide, heart disease affects about two-thirds of the affluent, killing about forty-five percent.

Doctors have had little success in preventing and curing heart disease by lowering cholesterol with medication. Reducing cholesterol with drugs have failed to decrease death rates, but statistically, have increased incidence of cancer and suicide. Lowering cholesterol with medication does not assure anyone they will escape heart disease.

The consumption of cholesterol in the U.S. has remained constant since 1900, but heart disease has increased dramatically between then and now. We can look back to the early 1900's and see that fat and sugar consumption was lower. The intake of minerals and vitamins was higher on diets that contained more vegetables and whole grains and less meat.

- SUGARS -

Since the beginning of the century, dramatic changes in food consumption in the U.S. have taken place. Fruits, grains and vegetables have been replaced by processed, nutritionally deficient, fatty foods and refined sugar.

In most cases, refined dietary sugars turn into fats, plus, starches can develop into saturated fats.

Cholesterol stickiness and saturated fats are just one factor in heart disease. Injury to the lining of the artery is caused due to toxic free radicals, oxidized LDL (low - density lipoprotein) cholesterol, oxidized triglyceride fatty acids, etc. By attempts at repair, they involve thickening the arteries by repair proteins apo(a) and fibrinogen, together with fats and cholesterol. With the combination of narrowed arteries and sticky platelets, heart attacks and strokes are waiting to happen. It's just a matter of time.

When natural sugar is refined and concentrated, the life force is dispersed and the natural balance is upset. When you stop eating sugar, your chances improve drastically in experiencing higher spirits, emotional stability, improved memory and speech, restful sleep and dreams, fewer colds and dental problems, more endurance and concentration and better health in general.

Soft drinks, cakes, cookies, confections, pies, many canned fruits and juices, jams and jellies, ice cream and deserts all contain hidden sugars and/or starches.

The next time you visit your grocery store, check out the sugar content in ketchup (huge amounts) along with other products that you use daily. Food products containing refined sugars increases your chances of stroke, heart attack, clogged arteries and diabetes.

When extra fats and cholesterol are produced from sugar, the body must get rid of the overload, by causing the excess fats to be deposited in the cells of the liver, heart, arteries, fat tissues, kidneys, muscles and other organs.

Vitamins and minerals required for metabolism is lacking in sugar products and must draw from the body's reserves for these nutrients. When these nutrients are depleted, the body cannot carry out other functions that require vitamins and minerals to be present to metabolize cholesterol and fats; the conversion of cholesterol into bile acids for removal from the body through the stool; or to burn-off excess fats as heat or increased activity. Due to this, cholesterol level increases; the metabolic rate is decreased; fats burn-off slower; we become lethargic and may become obese. Now, cardiovascular disease, diabetes and cancer is at risk due to obesity. With a decreased metabolic rate, the body is now involved with aging, arthritic diseases and cardiovascular disorders which is another general symptom of degenerative diseases.

The transport of vitamin C is interfered with by sugars because they use the same transport system. Sugar inhibits vitamin C's immune, virocidal, bactericidal, collagen and elastin-building, and tissue glue forming functions.

Sugars contribute considerably in causing fatty degeneration and degenerative disease by aiding the development of fat and cholesterol, thus, overloading the body; depleting the body's reserves of vitamins and minerals; interfering with essential fatty acid, adrenal gland, and immune systems functions; and by their lack of bulk and fiber. Also, sugar can cause damage to gallbladder and bowel function.

Sugars are considered by many researchers to be the major dietary cause of degenerative diseases. Refined sugar, perhaps more than any other common food, devastates the mineral condition of the body. They rob our body of minerals (especially chromium, potassium, magnesium and zinc) and vitamins (especially Bs).

Sugar producing triglycerides may create major health problems for the body, especially when the fats have been oxidized due to lack of antioxidant minerals and vitamins.

Exclusion of refined sugars from our diet slows aging and lengthens life span. Rats on calorie-restricted diets without sugar live fifty percent longer.

Sugar substitutes, such as aspartame (NutraSweet and Equal) should be excluded also. Symptoms associated with aspartame side effects can range from rashes, mild depression, headaches, nausea, ringing ears, vertigo, and insomnia to loss of motor control, loss or change of taste, slurred speech, memory loss, blurred vision, blindness, suicidal depression and seizures.

Saccharin (Sweet 'n Low) is an artificial sweetener. This additive is a possible human carcinogen.

-TRIGLYCERIDES-

Triglycerides store the body's reserves of essential fatty acids. These reserves are required for structure and function of the membranes and serve as precursors of prostaglandins and highly active, very highly unsaturated fatty acids required for the brain cells, synapses, retinas, adrenal glands and testes to function.

Problems may develop due to excess triglycerides. Our risk of heart disease is increased with levels of high blood triglycerides. This condition is produced by overeating and by high dietary intake of refined sugars, sticky saturated fats, and too few antioxidants. As a result, triglyceride fatty acids oxidize and damage the insides of the arteries, and high blood triglyceride levels may increase the tendency of clumping blood cells together.

In overweight or obese people, excess stored triglyceride fats correlate with high blood cholesterol and triglyceride levels. The risk of cardiovascular disease, high blood pressure, heart and kidney failure, cancer and other degenerative diseases is increased.

A diet rich in w3 fatty acids from flax oil can lower serum triglyceride levels by up to sixty-five percent. I experienced a sixty-four percent reduction. Folks who begin to take w3 oils sometimes will show remarkable reductions in their blood triglyceride and cholesterol levels.

Exercise will lower blood triglyceride levels by burning up excess fats to produce energy.

- HONEY -

Honey is one of the great foods and one of the great medicines. However, you *should not* eat honey with abandon. It is preferred you substitute honey for refined sugar. Honey is about thirty percent protein, and the rest is mostly carbohydrate in the form of a glucose-fructose (sugar) combination. Honey is sugar, and it is twice as sweet as white sugar and has more calories.

Use half as much honey as sugar and you still get a sweet taste. Another plus is raw, unheated, unprocessed honey contains small amounts of minerals, vitamins C, D, and E and some enzymes, therefore it doesn't throw the blood sugar out of balance to the degree that refined cane sugar does.

Raw honey is the only sweetener that reduces fatty accumulations in the vascular system - honey that is raw, unprocessed and unheated. Forget the supermarket when you shop for honey. Find it at your local health food store. It will be identified as "unfiltered" or "raw" on the label. Better yet, find a local bee keeper. This is what we have done. Our beekeeper has several areas where he keeps his bees, therefore, providing us with a choice of three different flavors. Buying honey locally supports small beekeepers and gives you the advantage of eating local pollens as a hedge against allergies.

The color and taste of honey will vary depending on the location of the pollen source. Color can range from dark, opaque and pungent, flowery and light to clear. Being a preservative, honey never spoils, but raw honey will harden after a few months. If this happens, place the jar in a pot of water and gently warm it until it liquefies.

Prior to the 1700's, honey and sugar were used more as medicines than foods and often to boost the immune system during a cold or flu by energizing the body and stimulating the adrenal glands. Since the industrial revolution, excessive amount of sugar (refined) eaten has the opposite effect of depressing the immune system.

Honey is a great substitute for sugar in baking. Use one half to three fourths the amount honey as you would sugar and decrease liquid by about one fourth cup. I use honey in my coffee substitute which I drink each morning. Be conservative whenever you use any intense sweetener. *It is not good to eat much honey. Proverbs 25:27.*

- REFINED FOODS -

The food industry removes important nutrients when food is refined to prevent spoilages. If food won't spoil, it can't be very nutritious. Nutritional therapists tell us to "eat things that spoil, but eat them before they do." Food refiners remove the wheat bran which contains seventeen nutrients: potassium, magnesium, zinc, calcium, manganese plus twelve more. They also remove ninety-six percent of one of the most powerful food antioxidants known - vitamin E.

Obesity, heart disease, stroke, breast cancer, prostate cancer, arthritis, osteoporosis, sexual dysfunction, immune dysfunction, birth defects, infertility, diabetes and depression follow the refined foods diet like night follows day. A few of the early warning signs that your diet is an enemy to your health are food allergies, indigestion, constipation, hemorrhoids, high blood pressure, weight gain, sinus infections, colds and flu.

Popping vitamin and mineral pills will not prevent the diseases associated with eating a refined food diet. Scientists cannot formulate into pills nutrients they haven't yet discovered.

Hippocrates said: *"Food should be your medicine, and medicine should be your food."* Scientists have proved him right.

It is not likely that refined, altered foods can bring together all the health benefits of nature's nutritional synergized whole foods. This is about as likely as your body being healthy without white blood cells.

By whole foods, we mean consuming a diet that is high in foods as whole as possible, with the least amount of processed, adulterated, fried, or sweetened additives. *It is whole foods, especially fresh fruits and vegetables, that pack the disease preventing wallop.*

Most plants and whole foods contain bioflavonoids. But processing often removes or destroys these helpers of heart, artery and liver health.

Healthy bodies must perform thousands of biochemical and psycho-chemical functions every minute. Only nature understands the nutritional science required to create perfect body fuels.

Mega-doses of vitamins and minerals cannot compensate for poor eating habits, nor can they make up for lack of fiber and missing phytochemicals (naturally occurring chemicals in plants that give fruits, vegetables, grains and legumes their medicinal, disease-preventing, health-enhancing properties).

Excessive amounts of fat and sugars in refined foods stimulate you to eat more calories than you can burn. Whole foods naturally contain less fat and sugar, therefore, you are inclined to consume fewer calories.

High blood sugar caused by refined foods triggers insulin surges to burn up excess energy. Unfortunately, insulin also encourages the body to store excess calories as fat and triglycerides.

Don't expect a refined food diet to curb your appetite in time to maintain your ideal weight. The best way to satisfy your body's nutritional needs and curb your appetite is to eat right. Eat whole foods which supply the building blocks the body needs to nourish and detoxify.

Of the refined, altered foods, white flour is one of the worst and is one of the reasons people are starving to death on full stomachs. It contains fifty percent less fiber than whole grain flour. Being a simple carbohydrate, the body converts it very quickly to sugar, therefore, adding to the problem of excess sugar consumption. White flour does not have the superior nutrition of whole grain flours which contain many fibers, vitamins, minerals and phytochemicals - uniquely balanced to energize your body.

Only the rich could afford to eat white fiberless flour prior to the industrial revolution. The process was slow and hard because it had to be hand-sifted. Due to this, only the wealthy, such as kings, noblemen and aristocrats, were subject to degenerative diseases that result from deficiencies of nutrients and fiber in white flour. The refined folks ate refined products while the poor folks ate whole grains. Poor folk's (common people) food was considered crude the same as their manners and upbringing was. The industrial revolution technology made refined foods available to everyone, rich and poor. The poor struggled to become "refined" and to be able to afford refined foods was a move up the social ladder. The results of degenerative diseases from the refined foods did not matter.

As I grew up during the depression of the 1930's, I often heard my dad make this comment after observing the condition of some of our neighbors: "Poor folks have poor ways."

We poor folks could be a lot healthier if the refined foods had remained solely for the rich.

- HYDROGENATION -

Hydrogenation is the most common way of drastically changing natural oils. Please be advised: DO NOT CONSUME any products that have hydrogenated oil of any kind! Hydrogenated oil is the worst kind of fat. These products contain large quantities of trans-fatty acids and other altered fat substances, some of which are known to be detrimental to health because they interfere with normal biochemical processes. Trans-fatty acids have now been shown to increase cholesterol, decrease beneficial HDL and interfere with our liver's detoxification system.

When you read food labels, you may often see a reference to "partially hydrogenated" oils. Partially hydrogenated oil contains more saturated fat. This alone is a good reason to make your own bread.

Please become a label reader. If health is your concern, hydrogenated products are unacceptable.

These trans-fatty acids act to inhibit other very necessary enzymes which help the body to form substances which reduces the stickiness of blood platelets. When blood platelets are sticky they tend to clump together, forming clots which easily plug up an artery already narrowed by plaque.

The process of hydrogenation changes the unsaturated and essential fatty acids present in a natural oil. Using a metal catalyst made from nickel, platinum or copper, natural oils are reacted under pressure with hydrogen gas at a temperature between 248 to 410 degrees F for six to eight hours.

"Raney's Nickel", a catalyst often used in this process, is fifty percent nickel and fifty percent aluminum. Traces of these two metals remain in products containing hydrogenated or partially hydrogenated oils and are consumed by people.

The presence of aluminum in the body is associated with Alzheimer's disease and osteoporosis and may also aid in the development of cancer.

Why do manufacturers use hydrogenation? It allows them to start with cheap, low-quality oils and to turn these into products that compete with butter in spreadability. Since margarines often taste slightly rancid, it cannot compete in taste.

Some oil chemists have said, "If the hydrogenation process were discovered today, it probably could not be adopted by the oil industry." The human body does not use these changed (hydrogenated) substances in the same way it uses natural fats and oils.

Due to the known and unknown effects that hydrogenation has on our health, government regulations passed to protect our health would forbid the use of this process for making edible products if it were introduced today. Since this process has been used commercially since the 1930s, it now has a long tradition established, hence, powerful oil lobbies in government continues to allow unnatural fat products in our foods.

The hydrogenation of oil to make margarines and shortenings, systematically and preferentially, destroys the only essential nutrients left in the oil. This results in a product that has had almost all of its essential nutrients deliberately removed or destroyed.

Margarine contains a man-made fat; hydrogenated vegetable oil. Researchers at Harvard estimate that at least thirty thousand Americans die every year as a result of the trans-fatty acids in margarine. The body is not equipped to handle this "plastic food" (*ants will not eat it!*) and it may ruin our blood vessels. It's an interesting fact that heart diseases first became common a few years after margarine was introduced.

There are non-fat margarines on the market which are a better choice, but there are a lot of unknown risks associated with eating so many food additives.

The chemical processing of fats destroys the vital electron cloud within the fat. Once the electrons have been removed, these fats can no longer bind with oxygen, and they actually become a harmful substance deposited within the body. The heart, for instance, rejects these fats, and they end up as inorganic fatty deposits on the heart muscle itself.

Margarine and shortening, furthermore, contain hydrogenated, polyunsaturated vegetable oils. Hydrogenation is an extremely harmful process that creates an immune-damaging synthetic fat, a type of trans-fatty acid that, to the dismay of confirmed margarine users, has also been found to actually elevate blood cholesterol. The use of butter is not recommended, however, butter is a better choice than margarine.

Hydrogenated vegetable oils that enter your diet are boxed cereals, most pastries and breads, which includes some whole wheat. Peanut butter is one of the worst culprits next to margarine; others are ice cream, fried foods, microwave meals, potato chips and corn chips. Probably half of all refined foods sold in containers contain hydrogenated vegetable oil. *Be a label reader!!*

- FATS/OILS -

Manufacturers want oils that will not spoil which are low in essential nutrients. Healers want oils that are good for us because they are EFA-rich, but these oils spoil easily.

Major damage occurs to our health when we depart from the fresh whole foods and the fresh, unaltered fats and oils that nature created for us.

When oil is refined, antioxidants, including vitamin E, are removed. The oil-refining industry does not throw away the vitamin E. They collect it and sell it at a profit.

The key word is natural. Man-made oils, such as hydrogenated oils and oils that have been tampered with by refining, are not good for you in any amount.

The fact is some fats heal and some fats kill. The results depend on what kind of fat it is, how it has been treated, is it fresh, has it been exposed to light, oxygen, heat, hydrogen and how old it is. How has it been used and how much was consumed?

There is no danger in cutting back on your consumption of fat. Virtually all natural foods contain some fat, such as fruits and vegetables. The body will make body fat from excess carbohydrates and protein. Fatty acid (linoleic acid) is the essential ingredient in our food, not the fat itself. The National Academy of Sciences reports that to stay healthy you need three to six grams per day, but new research suggests that the actual amounts of fatty acid (linoleic acid) the body needs could be as low as 0.1 percent of calories. One ounce of oatmeal or a slice of whole wheat bread will contain this much.

People often try to justify eating fat by saying their grandparents or great grandparents lived a long life with their high fat diet. First of all, not everyone will have cardiovascular disease. Second, their ancestors consumed very little refined foods. Also, oils you buy in the supermarket today are very different from those that people consumed many years ago.

Many problems develop with fat intake. If you do not want to wear your fat, don't eat it. The body converts one hundred calories of excess fat in food to ninety-seven calories of fat on bodies by burning just three measly calories.

Fat is an appetite stimulant. The more you eat the more you want. Fat adds calories 2.2 times faster than protein or carbohydrates. Insist on whole foods because they are naturally low in fat.

One hour after a fatty meal, blood cells begin to stick together. Within a six hour period the clumping is so severe that blood flow actually stops in small blood vessels. In addition to reducing the blood flow to the tissues, eating fatty food decreases the blood's oxygen supply by twenty percent. It is no wonder we feel tired after eating such a meal.

We believe that in order to reverse heart disease you need to avoid oil all together for at least two years (with the exception of flax oil). Also, *frying with oil is a no-no!* Frying is very damaging to our health regardless of the kind of oil you use.

Two of the most popular methods of "fast food" preparation is frying and deep-frying. This is also the two types of food preparation most damaging to health. Rapid oxidation and other chemical changes take place when oils are subjected to high temperature in the presence of light and oxygen. Antioxidants in the oil (vitamin E and carotene) are used up. Then, frying and deep-frying produce free radicals that start chain reactions in oil molecules and some trans-fatty acids are produced. Other oxidation products are far more toxic than trans-fatty acids. Frying and deep-frying produces scores of unnatural breakdown of molecules with unknown effects on health. Frying your food cannot be recommended for health.

- FLAXSEED OIL -

This is one fat that is actually good for you. Some fatty acids are considered more important than others because of their use by the body. Flaxseed oil contains both the essential fatty acids needed by the body, and is the highest concentration. Without sufficient EFA, cholesterol cannot be channeled and ends up as a sticky platelet on an artery wall. All whole, fresh, unprocessed foods contain some EFAs.

Certain illnesses, such as heart disease, require the optimum doses of flaxseed oil to counteract damage already done. It is not enough just to take flaxseed oil alone; you must have a good diet consisting of vitamin C, magnesium, zinc, B3 and B6. If you have a deficiency of these, the result will be poor utilization of the EFAs. Fresh flax oil, properly made, should be made a part of the entire population's diet.

Flax is excellent for digestive functions. EFAs are extremely important for health and vitality. EFA deficiencies are correlated with degenerative diseases such as cardiovascular disease, cancer, diabetes and various others.

Not only are flaxseeds richer in Omega 3's than fish oil, but they pack more fiber ounce for ounce than oat bran. Our body responds remarkable to the essential fatty acids. Omega 3 oils not only minimize circulatory disorders, but also encourage blood flow to tissues damaged by lack of circulation. Omega 3 oils lower triglyceride levels by up to sixty-five percent, and high cholesterol by twenty-five percent. They also reduce clotting.

Interestingly, Omega 3's used to be found in beef back in the days when cattle grazed on native grasses and plants instead of being stuffed with corn, estrogen, antibiotics and who knows what else. This may be one reason our ancestors could have meat in their diet and not suffer from heart disease. Flaxseed, with its rich concentration of essential fatty acids, is truly a dietary need whose time has come.

Not all flax oil is created equal. We believe the highest quality flax oil available is Barlean's. The reason: the Barlean's take great care in making sure their flax oil provides the benefits mother nature intended. They do this by using one hundred percent certified organic flaxseed and then expelling the oil through a special procedure called the "Bio-Electron Process."   This process allows the oil to be expressed at a temperature below ninety-six degrees Fahrenheit and protects the oil from the damaging effects of heat, light and oxygen. You can actually taste the difference in quality of Barlean's to other flax oils. Be sure to buy plain flax oil (the label will be in black). An excellent way to use flax oil is in making homemade salad dressings (see Flax Dressing in recipe section).

A diet high in saturated fat has been linked to many chronic diseases while a diet low in saturated fat, but high in essential fatty acids, prevents the very same diseases.

Flax is rapidly becoming a wonder grain for health. The fresh oil of the most useful flax seed is the w3-richest edible oil we know. Fresh, it has a light and nutty taste that is delightful. It is much lighter than commercial oils which have a heavy, oily texture.

People go to great lengths to get flaxseed oil air-shipped fresh. This is because fresh flax oil spoils when exposed to light, oxygen and heat, therefore, care needs to be taken in pressing, filling, storing and shipping. If this care is not taken, fresh flax oil turns into rancid linseed oil which should be discarded. Flax oil needs to be refrigerated at all times and used within six weeks after opening.

Flax seeds are protected by a tough seed coat, therefore, if swallowed whole, your body will not get the nutrients they contain. After the seeds pass through your digestion system, you could plant them, and they would still grow. Grind whole flax seeds in a small coffee grinder which you can purchase for about twelve dollars. This will break the seed coat and make the nutrients accessible for digestion. This way you get the freshest, best-tasting, least spoiled oil possible plus all of the other nutrients contained in flax. Seeds should be ground shortly before eating, and grind only the amount you plan to use. Once seeds are exposed to air, they begin to spoil very quickly.

Flax seeds are rich in antioxidants, vitamins and minerals.

Freshly ground flax should be taken with plenty of fluid, because its mucilage absorbs five times the seed's weight of water. Use from one to six tablespoons per day. One tablespoon of flax contains about one teaspoon of oil; six tablespoons of flax contain two tablespoons of oil.

The use of freshly ground flax seeds can improve digestion, prevent and reverse constipation, stabilize blood glucose levels, improve cardiovascular health, inhibit tumor formation and bring about many other beneficial effects.

Flax oil is a powerful traditional, clinical and therapeutic toll against cardiovascular disease, cancer, diabetes, arthritis and other degenerative diseases.

A unique feature of flax seed is that it may contain a substance resembling prostaglandins that regulate blood pressure, platelet, kidney, immune and arterial function, inflammatory response and play key roles in calcium and energy metabolism.

Flax oil (fresh-unrefined) contains lecithin and other phospholipids that aid in emulsifying fats and oils for easier digestion and contributes to physical health. Also, it contains beta carotene (pro-vitamin A) and vitamin E which is necessary to stabilize the oil in both bottle and body. Refining oil removes vitamins and lecithin, plus, it loses its stability and many health-giving minor components.

Avoid ground flax meal sold in plastic containers in stores. It's usually rancid. Fresh flax oil exposed to light and air loses its fresh taste within a matter of a few days.

Dr. Johanna Budwig, a seven time Nobel Prize nominee, is famous for flaxseed oil findings. She is known and highly respected around the world as Germany's premier biochemist. In addition, Dr. Budwig holds a Ph.D. in Natural Science, has undergone medical training and was schooled in pharmaceutical science, physics, botany and biology.

She is best known for her extensive research on the properties and benefits of flaxseed oil combined with sulphurated proteins (in cottage cheese) in the diet, and over the years has published a number of books on the subject, including *True Health Against Arteriosclerosis* and *Heart Infarction & Cancer*.

Dr. Budwig has assisted many seriously ill individuals, even those given up as terminal by orthodox medical practitioners, to regain their health through a simple regimen of nutrition. The basis of Dr. Budwig's program is the use of flaxseed oil blended with low-fat cottage cheese. Her research was based on using the ratio of two tablespoons flaxseed oil mixed with one fourth cup of low-fat cottage cheese.

Dr. Budwig has endorsed BioSan C-Leinosan Flaxseed Oil, made by Barlean's Organic Oils (1-800-445-FLAX) which is available at your health food store (usually in a special refrigerated section) or by mail.

It is important to include flax oil in our diet due to the poor oil and food choices that have taken hold in affluent western societies. Too much emphasis has been placed on protein-rich foods and the removal or over-processing of spoilable w3 oils from our food supply creates this need. Flax oil, the w3-richest food available, redresses this nutritional imbalance between proteins in our foods and good oils.

You will only need to use this oil until your body has had its w3 supply replenished and you are healthy which should be within six months to one year.

For a tasty snack, Joy likes diced apples with cottage cheese and flax oil. I prefer the flax oil dressing (see recipe section pages 145 and 218) used as a dip for home made bread.

Note: Use fresh flax straight from the refrigerator, and make sure each bottle is used within three to six weeks after opening. A stock of oil can be kept frozen solid in a freezer, where it will remain fresh for over a year.

All oil starts to go rancid on contact with air. Keeping the lid on tightly does not prevent damage, because air enters the bottle as soon as it is opened.

While one teaspoon to two tablespoons per day of flax oil is sufficient for healthy people, those with degenerative conditions should take two to three tablespoons per day.

Flax oil can be used on hot vegetables, in hot cereals, on pasta, in mashed potatoes, on toast but added just before eating.

Also, it can be used in bread - the inside of bread is protected from light and oxygen and is cooked at a safe temperature.

Flax oil should *never* be used for frying.

- MILK -

Milk rates second only to beef as the largest source of saturated fat in the American diet. Whole milk is sometimes called 3.5 percent fat which doesn't sound too bad until you realize that it's 3.5 percent of the total weight, and most of the weight is water. Almost fifty percent of the calories of whole milk are from fat.

"Low-fat milk," also referred to as two percent fat, actually has thirty-five percent of calories as fat. Non-fat milk, also called skim milk, has less than 2.5 percent of the calories as fat.

Milk is one of the most over-rated, over-hyped foods in America. Unless you drink skim milk, you are drinking a product that is very high in fat. Twenty-two percent of the calories in "low" fat milk come from saturated fat. In summary, thirty-five percent of the calories in "low" fat milk are from fat. The low refers to the percentage of fat by weight.

Non-organic milk contains residues of antibiotics. Drugs are routinely added to animal feed. This drug practice is very alarming. If you drink milk regularly, you are getting a very low dose of antibiotics. It is not enough to kill bacteria. The bacteria soon becomes resistant to the drugs.

After the age of twelve, most people lose the enzymes to digest milk. This is why many adults experience gas or indigestion after drinking a glass of milk. Are you struggling with fatigue, battling frequent colds, or fighting chronic sinus congestion? Extract milk from your diet and get ready for a pleasant surprise.

Don't expect to get calcium from milk; it doesn't contain enough magnesium to get a good amount of the calcium into your bones. Many vegetables are a great source of calcium. One cup of kale has more absorbable calcium than a glass of milk.

Your best sources for calcium is fresh vegetables and legumes. They may not have as high of a concentration of this mineral as dairy products do, but they have it in a more readily absorbable form.

What can you put on your cereal instead of dairy milk? We use soy milk. Soybeans lower cholesterol. Soy also contains substances that can balance hormones in the body. Eating more soy appears to have a protective effect against breast and prostate cancers. Rice milk works well for people who are highly allergic.

Soy milk comes in plain or original, vanilla and carob or chocolate flavors. Our favorite is the WestSoy non-fat or low-fat vanilla. On cereal it's better than milk, especially when you add one to two tablespoons of lecithin granules.

Health food stores will carry all of these milks. Unopened, the milk stays good for months. All of these products are organic.

- FIBER -

Fiber is a powerful cell cleanser and waste remover. Fiber pulp expel toxic wastes with less delay which protects against internal toxemia. This dynamic cleansing action makes fiber unique in its healing powers. Since excess cholesterol may be labeled as waste, it is important to use fiber to sweep it out.

The use of fresh, raw and unprocessed foods is essential for boasting the benefits of cleansing fiber. Refined, processed foods offer minimal amounts of essential roughage.

Good sources of fiber are whole grains, vegetables (raw is preferred), fruits with edible seeds and skins, and green peas, dried beans and peas, lentils and lima beans.

One of the very best sources of natural fiber is figs. The single most concentration of fiber is in bran - the outer husk of grains. Flax is another excellent source of fiber.

Pure bran passes down into your lower bowel, absorbs water, adds bulk, then promotes a scouring-cleansing-detoxifying action throughout this entire region.

Pectin, a fiber found in apples, cherries, bananas and other fruits, eliminates cholesterol from the digestive track.

The absence of sufficient fiber in refined carbohydrates slows down the digestive process as the food travels through the digestive tract. This causes this waste material to remain in our colon much too long, thereby, causing a source of food for harmful bacteria that produces gas and toxins and can cause the colon to become inflamed and ballooned. Constipation is a result due to lack of fiber, and it is so consistent in this effect that white (fiber-deficient) bread was used in the 1800's to stop diarrhea because of its reliability in plugging up the colon. Other problems which result from lack of fiber are; liver-weakening toxin reabsorption, hemorrhoids and varicose veins, and encourages the development of bowel cancer. A high fiber diet will help remove excess cholesterol and bile acids from the body; thus preventing their reabsorption and recirculation.

Diets that are predominantly plant-based are nutrient-rich, high in fiber and low in fat content. Eat less animal fat and protein and eat more fiber. Doing so will protect you against cancer, especially cancer of the colon. Research studies indicate that adding fiber to your diet shrinks pre-cancerous polyps in the lower colon, thereby, reducing your cancer risk.

When your dietary fiber is adequate your bowels empty sooner, which reduces fermentation and normalizes the pH balance. Soluble fiber helps to lower your cholesterol and prevents the liver from recycling bile. This forces the body to continually make new bile. Cholesterol, taken from your blood stream, is a major ingredient the body uses in making bile.

Absence of sufficient fiber will allow food to ferment too long in the colon causing harmful pH conditions. Bile acids become carcinogenic and create problems. Abnormal pH readings are common in cancer patients.

Digestive processes naturally produce chemicals that, when left in the body too long, can poison you. Fiber absorbs these like a sponge and flushes them from the body.

According to Bernard Jensen, one of the best-known natural healers alive today, many degenerative diseases start in our colon through the toxic effects of constipation.

All beans are an excellent source of fiber. Even though some nutrients are lost during processing, canned beans may be used.

Bran has over nine grams of fiber in only three and one half ounces. Make a "bran shaker" and keep it on your table to sprinkle it over your food. Add it to stews and casseroles.

Plant fiber, particularly that in whole grains, helps to reduce fat in the blood and prevent hardening of the arteries.

A high-fiber vegetarian diet can lower a cholesterol level by a significant amount within a month and also supplies an abundance of antioxidants, minerals and vitamins.

- PROTEIN -

Protein means "primary substance." All the tissues of the body are built and repaired with protein. Amino acids, the building blocks of protein, are key factors in most of the processes and functions of the body. Protein is a basic component in the antibodies of the immune system, the hemoglobin of red blood cells, most hormones and all enzymes.

The daily protein requirement of a one hundred seventy pound man doing light work is twenty-five to thirty grams. A bowl of pea or bean soup, a slice of whole grain bread and a vegetable salad supplies all the protein he needs.

Beans and rice together are a complete protein and a good substitute for meat. Egg whites are another good source of protein.

Over-consumption of protein is more common than under-consumption. Too much protein overtaxes the system.

-WATER-

It is important to drink only clean water. There is a forty percent chance that our drinking water will have passed through someone's sewer or as industrial conduit filled with waste, poisons and bacteria. Most cities add chlorine to disinfect the water.

Chlorine has been shown to have an effect on the arteries, and fluoride lowers thyroid function which in turn allows levels of cholesterol and homocysteine (a free radical generator capable of oxidizing cholesterol, one of the major contributing factors in heart disease) to rise.

Once out of the tap, chlorine evaporates. Many people draw chlorinated water and let it stand at least thirty minutes. Unfortunately, chlorine combines with any organic substances that may be in the water to form chloroform, a poisonous cancer-causing chemical which does not evaporate.

When chlorine is regularly ingested, it destroys vitamin E in the body and its presence is closely linked with vascular disease. It will also destroy beneficial flora in the intestines. Chlorine is considered a hazard even on the surface of the body. The Environmental Protection Agency has warned that prolonged swimming or bathing in chlorinated water contributes to skin cancer.

Fluoridated water is used by more than half of the cities in America. Although many ailments and disorders have been linked to fluoridated water such as Down's syndrome, mottled teeth and cancer, fluoridation has become the standard rather than the exception. Fluoridation also damages the immune system and increases other degenerative conditions. Fluoride in common drinking water increases the risk of hip fracture. Fluoride is toxic to bone cells.

Steam distilled water is a good water to drink. One way you can add a better flavor is to add one or two tablespoons of raw apple cider vinegar (obtained from a health food store) to one gallon of water.

Another good way to have clean water is to purchase a reverse osmosis purifier (we installed our own R-0 unit). These membranous units take out nearly all toxins, gases and minerals, (including chlorine and fluoride) leaving almost completely purified water. They were very expensive at one time but now are competitively priced. There are several available. We purchased one from Kelco Water Engineering, Inc., Yuma, Arizona (1-800-365-3526). They are easily installed under your kitchen sink.

-SALT-

Salt does not allow the blood to circulate properly and too much salt in the system can cause excessive fluid build-up. It should be used sparingly. You will soon enjoy the flavor of food more when you restrict your salt intake. We use sea salt. It tastes the same but contains trace minerals such as; magnesium, calcium and potassium. Sea salt is sold at your health food stores.

-ORGANIC FOODS-

To reduce our intake of pesticides, we must avoid sprayed foods and return to pesticide free foods - organically grown fresh vegetables, fruits and whole grains. These foods kept our ancestors free of fat related diseases and will also keep us healthy.

Farmers spray seven hundred and fifty million pounds of pesticides annually on their corps, and synthetic fertilizers are used at twenty-two billion pounds per year.

Buying food that is organically grown insures you of much healthier eating and helps save our country's top soil. Soil that is treated with chemical fertilizers makes the soil more vulnerable to erosion. Four million acres of cropland have been lost through erosion. Please purchase organic products when possible. Your body will thank you.

-MEATS-

All kinds of meats are likely to contain bacteria that infect the intestines, causing colitis and many other diseases. Meats always cause putrefaction.

Meat purchased at fast food restaurants have caused many people to become sick from undercooked contaminated food. Some have died from this food poisoning. This is caused by a mutant strain of E. coli bacteria. This mutant strain is both toxic and resistant to antibiotics. It is an overuse of antibiotics that has caused this new strain. Antibiotics are routinely fed to cattle to fight infection and to fatten them up for slaughter.

Unfortunately, these low-level doses, in addition to causing weight gain, also cause bacteria normally present in the cattle to undergo a mutation and develop a resistance to the antibiotics.

This is a serious problem and may get worse. A study reported in the *Journal of the American Medical Association* estimates that "more than fifty percent of what we call 'stomach flu' is not flu at all, but instead is bacteria-induced food poisoning as a consequence of contamination of our food with new 'super bugs.'"

A meat diet will cause cancer in some cases. Research has proved this; thereby removing any doubt.

When a person consumes too much meat, excessive uric acid is developed and this may cause rheumatism, Bright's disease, kidney stones, gout and gallstones. Excessive uric acid in your system can be reduced by a diet of potatoes.

Meat protein causes putrefaction twice as fast as vegetable protein. Vegetable products can produce every ingredient (except vitamin B12) that meat produces. A second-hand food product, such as meat, will not make healthy, pure blood or form good tissues. Protein is plentiful in beans, peas, lentils, nuts of all kinds and soybeans. In this light, meat is not a necessary food to obtain protein.

Red meat is a source of homocysteine-generating fat.

Remember Methuselah? This Bible patriarch lived to be nine hundred and sixty-nine years of age. A life of nine hundred years for man during this time was common. When man's diet included flesh, introduced sometime after the great flood, life expectancy decreased to a little over one hundred years.

The muscle from animals is the most common part that is consumed. This section of meat has varying amounts of fat and other tissues such as nerves and blood vessels, as well as many toxic substances that are not seen. All of the vital processes that were taking place in the animal stopped abruptly when it was slaughtered. Toxins that were in the tissues at death remained. Some of these are; urea, uric acid, creatinine, creatine, phenolic acid, adrenaline, possibly various bacteria and parasites, either dead or alive, various hormones, antibiotics, pesticides, herbicides, and other elements the animal had been exposed to or eaten while alive.

Fish in some areas contain a certain amount of chemicals such as lead, mercury, calcium, cadmium, zinc, antimony and arsenic. When pesticides, such as DDT, are introduced to the body, they become very slowly degradable, thereby accumulating in the fat and muscles of animals. Fish, poultry and meat contribute thirteen times more DDT to the average diet than vegetables.

Cooking one pound of steak well done on your charcoal broiler will produce four to five micrograms of benzopyrene, an amount equal to what you would get from smoking about three hundred cigarettes. Cooked fat from the meat drips onto the charcoal producing benzopyrene that distills back up onto the meat. Benzopyrene is one of the main cancer-producing agents found in tobacco smoke.

All fried and broiled foods contain mutagens, chemicals that can damage cellular reproductive material. But fried and broiled meats have far more mutagens than similarly prepared plant foods. One study indicates that some twenty percent of American meat eaters may have toxic mutagens in their digestive tracts that can be absorbed into the blood stream where they can attack cells. The same study indicates that vegetarians are unlikely to have any mutagens in their digestive tracts.

The danger of cancer is enhanced with food additives, such as nitrites, that are used in some meats to help keep a healthy, fresh, pink color. These nitrites may be changed to nitrosamines that are highly carcinogenic.

Proteins from animal products will change the way some bacteria act in our intestines. Bile acids are changed by these bacteria into potential cancer-forming compounds, and a meat diet (low-fiber) promotes constipation and prolongs the contact of these toxic compounds with the lining membrane of the colon, therefore, promoting the development and growth of colon tumors.

A visit to the feedlots, slaughterhouses and chicken farms, where you could see how the animals you eat were fed and slaughtered (particularly the way meat is handled after the slaughter), might change your way of thinking about eating meat.

-BREAD-

Bread made from whole grain flours has been the staff of life since early Bible times. One way to guarantee that you get the very best is to make it yourself. Breads made from whole grains are high in fiber, B-complex vitamins, minerals and a good source of complex carbohydrates. They taste full and rich and satisfying, just the way God intended for it to be.

The stuff that food companies pack in plastic bags and call "bread" is useless food made with vitamin-poor bleached white (refined) flour. Even when the label says "wheat flour" it means "white flour". Only when the ingredient list says "whole wheat flour" are you getting any whole-grain flour. Plus, we have never found one without partially hydrogenated oil. Read the label!

Making breads from whole grains is a great way to start changing to a more healthy way of eating. A bread machine is an easy way to do this. It only takes five minutes to put on a loaf of bread with this machine. There is nothing to compare with the taste and smell of hot , fresh bread - yummy!

Make sure you purchase one hundred percent whole wheat flour.

We believe one of the best bread machines on the market is "The Breadman". It was rated number one by the Consumer's Report and is available in two sizes and can be found in most large department stores.

There is a book, *The Breadman's Healthy Bread Book* by George Burnett, which you will find at your local book store. It's great! His recipes contain different oils. We substitute with flax oil.

TIP: Purchase a bread slicing guide and electric knife. This makes slicing so much easier.

Remember - *You are what you eat!*

-CAFFEINE-

Caffeine was my hardest obstacle to overcome when I started my low-fat vegetarian diet. Oh how I loved that first cup of coffee every morning. I was not what you would call a heavy coffee drinker. I rarely had more than two cups daily. In most cases it was only that one cup the first thing every morning, but still, I was hooked on this stimulant.

When you drink a cup of coffee, the caffeine chemically stimulates your sympathetic nervous system. Your level of adrenalin and other stress hormones quickly begins to rise. Caffeine and other stimulants increase the risk of coronary heart disease. Also, they can increase the frequency and severity of irregular heartbeats. Caffeine will potentiate the stress response - giving you a short fuse.

Other products that contain caffeine are colas, chocolate and other cocoa products, regular teas and in many over-the-counter medications (Excedrin, diet pills, and many others). Decaffeinated coffees, teas and soft drinks still contain some caffeine.

After considering the effects that caffeine was having on my body, it didn't take long for me to make a change in the right direction. This meant finding a good coffee substitute.

During my search for a coffee substitute, I found several that are very tasty. You will find them at your local health food store. Pero, Roma, Cafix and Postum are just a few. My favorite is Pero. The ingredients of this beverage are: malted barley, barley, chicory and rye. Don't expect these drinks to taste like coffee. They have their own distinct flavor and best of all, they are one hundred percent caffeine free.

He who has no time for health today may have no health for time tomorrow.

CHAPTER THREE - EXERCISE/WALKING-YOGA

You should be ready to start your own program to reverse heart disease and have a better and healthier life. I will explain the program that reversed my heart disease. This is a proven program. If followed, you could also have the same results.

> 1. Daily Walking Exercise
> 2. Daily Yoga Exercise
> 3. Low-Fat Vegetarian Diet

To get started, you must have a sound exercise and low-fat vegetarian diet program. The combination of the two, exercise and low-fat vegetarian diet, must be done together with a precise schedule that will fit into you own program, one that you are comfortable with and can maintain daily, weekly and monthly. Set up a daily schedule that you can adhere to. Take one day at a time. This is how goals are accomplished.

Everyone has a schedule they normally go through daily. We get out of bed. We eat breakfast. We brush our teeth, take a shower and go to work. Not necessarily in that order. But everyone has a daily schedule, good or bad, which is performed daily.

Get your priorities straight. Outline a schedule you can live by and stick with it. It is always good to have your wife/husband or a partner to get involved with you in an exercise program. This is an excellent support system and between the two of you, can keep the program on track.

This support system has worked extremely well for us. Many days we had the urge not to take our daily walk. However, in each case one encouraged the other. "Get your walking shoes on and let's go!"

You may already have a walking program in place. This is good. Most heart patients do walk.

Our walking program is forty-five to fifty minutes, covering approximately three miles. This averages out to be about sixteen minutes per mile, which is very brisk. However, it is not necessary to cover this distance (three miles) in this time span; it just happens to be our normal speed in walking.

After my bypass surgery in 1981, it was my goal to walk one mile in twelve minutes. After weeks of practice and extreme endurance, I accomplished this goal. I think back on that experience now and it seems very foolish of me to put my body through such torture - and it was torture. Have you ever tried walking a mile in twelve minutes? Try it sometime. If you are twenty years old, that's not fair. If you are over fifty, this puts you in my league and you will experience the difficulty and the strain on your body. Wait until you have been on a low-fat vegetarian diet for several months before you undertake such trivial matters if you are so inclined.

Walk every day if possible. A minimum of walking three days a week should be established. Your walk can be at anytime during the day or night, whatever fits your schedule. The distance you walk should not matter; just as long as you walk for at least thirty-five to forty minutes. It is suggested that you not "stroll", but maintain a good pace, one that stimulates the body. In other words, get the "blood flowing".

Regular exercising is the most significant factor in attaining, maintaining and restoring health. When you have a realistic exercise program it will prolong your life and make the difference between feeling tired and old, and feeling full of energy and great. No matter what your age, it is essential for everyone to exercise. Walking has become our choice of exercise. Brisk walking can be fun and relaxing. Joy and I use this period of time to discuss whatever is on our mind. Walking together is certainly quality time spent with my spouse.

-PRIMARY WALKING PROCEDURE-

A good walking posture is obtained when you stand up straight and walk with your ears, shoulders, hips, knees and ankles in a vertical line. Your head should be kept erect with your chin pulled in toward your neck, back straight and buttocks and stomach tucked in. Do not lean forward as you walk (some people do when they are trying to walk faster). Doing so may cause back strain.

As you walk, look forward and focus your eyes about fifteen to twenty feet ahead of you. Eliminate walking on rough terrain that forces you to watch your feet.

Your shoulders should be relaxed and directly above your hips, not slumped forward or raised up toward your ears. Bend your arms at the elbow at ninety degrees, with wrists straight and fingers gently curled into a loose fist. A straight-arm swing can result in swollen fingers and a slower pace. Your bent arms should swing in a straight line from front to back, close to your body, with the hand opposite the forward leg rising to chest level while the other hand moves back parallel to the hip.

A full stride should be taken, letting your legs be your locomotive. The stride should be made with knees straight and with the forward leg directly in front of the body. If your size and shape permit, you should end up walking with one foot in front of the other in a single straight line. Walk heel to toe, letting your foot roll gently forward through each step. Maintain a rhythmic cadence, stopping as little as possible.

If you already have a proper stride and wish to increase your speed, step more frequently rather than trying to stretch your stride, which can injure your knees.

When walking up a step hill, you have no choice but to lean into the hill, but you can still keep your back straight, eyes forward and chin in. Shorten your stride, your knees will remain bent and, if the incline is rather steep, more of your weight will be on the balls of your feet.

Be sure to stretch before and after your walk (I do my yoga exercises prior to walking). The American Physical Therapy Association recommends side bends and trunk rotations (turning the upper body while feet remain planted) as well as leg stretches for the inner thigh, calf muscles, quadriceps and hamstring.

It is important to wear good walking shoes that have flexible, non-sticky soles, good arch supports, cushioned insoles, heel cushions that are about one-half to three-quarters of an inch thick, and roomy toe boxes. If your socks get holes in the toes, your shoes do not fit properly; either they are too short or your foot is sliding forward with each step. If your walking shoes wear unevenly or if you develop discomfort in your feet, knees or hips, orthotic inserts in your shoes might help. If these problems occur you might consider consulting a sports medicine specialist.

Adding weights to your walking is not recommended. Ankle weights can strain the knees and increase the risk of tripping. Hand weights can strain your elbows. Walking on grass (or firm cushioned surface), wood floors (featured at some athletic clubs) or asphalt is a better choice than walking on concert.

-YOGA-

In addition to a walking program, I suggest that you incorporate some form of yoga exercises. Yoga exercises are nonstrenous. Older people can find a plan that won't cause undue fatigue. I have used a form of yoga for three years and it continues to be a part of my program.

Yoga is the oldest known science of self-development. It is mental, physical and spiritual control. Developed thousands of years ago in India, yoga literally means joining. The joining of the individual self with the universal self. Joining is achieved through the practice and mastering of specific physical postures, call asanas, breathing exercises called pranayama, and meditation, what is known as the path of Raja Yoga, and its subdivision, Hatha Yoga. These are the two most popular yoga systems - Hatha Yoga (physical practice), Raja Yoga (mental exercise).

At the beginning of my program I was not enthused about doing yoga. My lack of knowledge in yoga gave me a mind-set in a negative manner. I previously thought of yoga as some sort of religion. However, yoga is not designed for any particular technique, religion, or philosophy - yoga is not a religion. Further study of the subject opened my eyes. I was searching for any sound program to reverse my diseased heart. After establishing several postures that I was comfortable with, this daily routine is something that I look forward to each morning.

Yoga allows us to increase our awareness. This extends our control over what is happening within our body. The result is, we can notice the effects of stress and make changes before they develop into a degenerative condition such as heart disease.

The stretching exercises will help to loosen up chronically tensed muscles. The meditation and breathing techniques help you become more aware of situations in which you are stressed and they give you the method to do something about it.

The various postures is a technique that will help quiet down your mind and body, therefore, allowing you to experience an inner sense of relaxation, peace and joy. This is a natural state that you were born with when your body and mind reaches this tranquil condition.

After you have completed your session of yoga postures, remind yourself that this feeling of relaxation, peace and joy did not come from anywhere outside you; it was already there. You purged out some of the physical and emotional stress that may have kept you from feeling that way all the time.

Your body and mind will function more efficiently and effectively when you are relaxed. When you manage stress more effectively, you can accomplish more.

The yoga postures should be performed slowly and gently, with grace and control, as a type of meditation rather than as a form of calisthenics.

Learning to stretch and lengthen muscles that are chronically contracted helps to rebalance both your body and mind. The point is not to see how far you can stretch, but rather just to stretch as far as feels comfortable for you. Pay attention to how you are feeling and stretch accordingly, not to what you think you should be doing.

Slowly and gently stretch chronically tensed muscles. Allow your body to relax. Forcing muscles to lengthen may agitate the tensed muscles, making conditions worse. Your movements should be unforced and gentle as you develop a smooth routine. The more time you devote to your postures, the more benefits you receive.

Your period of relaxation between postures is just as important as the postures themselves.

As you progress, you do not need to learn more advanced positions; just hold these positions a little longer.

You can do your yoga postures at any time. I choose the early part of the day. The early morning is peaceful. My neighborhood is quiet. My house is quiet and my yoga room is quiet. My body is relaxed and I am ready to begin with each posture.

Before you begin your yoga exercise, be sure that you are dressed in comfortable, loose fitting clothes.

Start with Posture # 1-Resting Position.

POSTURE # 1 - *Resting Position*

This is one of the most important postures for compound or entire body effect. Lie on your back, arms to the side, with palms facing up. Legs are about eighteen inches apart. Close your eyes. Let yourself go. Allow your muscles to relax so that you're not using any muscles to hold them in position. The focus is relaxation, total calmness, harmony, and peace. The resting position can also be performed while lying on your abdomen.

POSTURE # 2 - *Knee Squeeze*
Lay on your back flat on the floor. Bend your right knee and slowly bring it up to your chest. Grasp your knee with both hands and slowly pull it to your chest. The left leg remains on the floor. Feel the stretch in your lower back and in the left hip. Then repeat with the left leg, then with both legs. Repeat each exercise four times.

POSTURE # 3 - *Shoulder Stand*

*Lie on your back with your feet together and your arms
alongside your body, palms down. Inhale, straighten
your legs and lift them over your head in a horizontal
position. Begin breathing normally.*

POSTURE # 4 - *Shoulder Stand*

While still in the # 3 Posture, bring your palms to your lower back for support and gradually straighten your legs to a vertical position, bringing your chin and your chest close together. Continue breathing normally. When you're ready, slowly lower your legs over your head again so they are parallel to the floor, transfer your forearms to the floor, and bring your trunk down slowly, then lower your legs to the floor.

POSTURE # 5 - Fish Pose

Lie on your back. Bring your legs together and grasp the sides of your thighs. Rest your weight on your elbows. Raise your head and trunk to a half-seated position. Arch the back, thrusting out the chest. Lower your head and place the top of your head on the floor. Balance your weight between the elbows, the top of your head, and your buttocks. Smile, this will relax any tension in your jaw. To return to relaxing position, shift your weight to your elbows, straighten your neck and back, and then lower yourself down to the floor. The fish pose helps to release any tension caused by the shoulder stand.

POSTURE # 6 - *Back Stretch (Cobra Pose)*
Lie on your abdomen. Rest your forehead on the floor. Place your palms on the floor beneath your shoulders, with your fingers pointing forward and your elbows raised and close to your body, as if you were going to do a push-up. Your legs are together and your toes pointed. Inhale and stretch your chin forward and without pushing down on your hands, slowly raise your head, neck, and chest off the floor. Keep your pelvis on the floor and breath normally.

Hold this position for a few seconds. Repeat it two to four times. Exhale as you slowly roll down, touching your chin, then your forehead, then your shoulders to the floor. Turn your cheek to the side leaving your hands in place. Gradually increase the time (about one minute) that you spend in this position. As you come down to return to resting position, turn your cheek to the side, release your arms and legs, and spend a few seconds in the resting position on your abdomen.

The Cobra Pose affects the sympathetic nervous system and the nervous system as a whole. The muscles of the shoulders, neck, and back, flexibility of the spine, elasticity of the lungs, and circulation around the vertebrae are also all enhanced. This pose focuses on the spine and back.

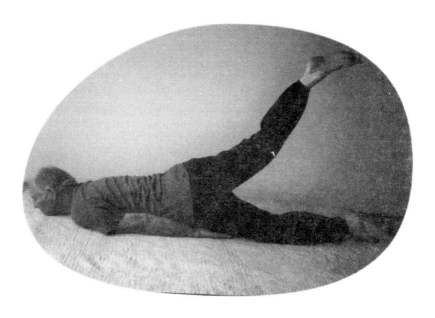

POSTURE # 7 - Half Locust Pose

Lie down on your abdomen with your chin on the floor. Push your arms underneath your body, with your elbows close under your body and your palms facing your thighs. Keep your pelvis on your arms. Inhale, straighten your right leg and slowly raise if off the floor as far as you feel comfortable. Up to ten seconds hold this position, breathing normally, then slowly lower your leg. Do this several times with each leg.

POSTURE # 8 - *Full Locust Pose*
Same as # 7. Inhale to stiffen the body, keep your chin on the floor, and raise both legs together at a comfortable distance without bending your knees. Breathe normally and repeat several times for ten seconds each time.

POSTURE # 9 - Forward Stretch-One

Sit on the floor with both legs stretched out in front of you. Bend your left leg and place the sole of your left foot against the inside of your right thigh. Curl your toes back to keep your right knee straight. Inhale, look up, lock your thumbs, and raise your arms overhead as far as you comfortably can. Exhale, bending forward from the hips, keeping your back straight. Grasp your foot, ankle with both hands and bring your head down as far as you can. Allow the head to rest, and breathe normally. Hold position for several deep breaths. Repeat this with your other leg. Repeat several times with each leg. Slowly come back to the starting position. The muscles of the back and hamstrings are affected.

POSTURE # 10 - *Forward Stretch - Two*
Same pose as Forward Stretch - One. Instead of bending one leg, stretch out over both legs together. Reach up before bending forward.

POSTURE # 11 - The Twist

Sit with legs straight out in front of you. Cross your left foot over your right knee, placing the sole of your left foot flat on the floor. Sit up straight. Bring your left knee close to your chest. Extend your arms in front of you, lock your thumbs, and twist to the left. Unlock your thumbs and place your left hand on the floor behind you, close to your body, with your fingers pointing away from you. Place your right arm between your trunk and your left knee, and press your knee to the left. Reach around your left knee with your right hand and grasp the outside of your right leg or the instep of your left foot. Slowly twist your head and trunk to the left and look over your left shoulder. After 20 to 60 seconds, slowly unwind and do the same pose on the other side. The entire spine is affected in this posture.

POSTURE # 12 - Kneeling

Sit in a kneeling position. Keep the head and trunk straight. Place the hands on the knees with palms facing down. Sit on your inner soles, toes touching, with heels pointed out.

POSTURE # 13 - *Modified Chest Expansion*

Sit in a kneeling position and sit on your heels, or a cross-legged position. Bring your arms behind your back, and interlock your fingers. Inhale and bend forward at the waist, at the same time raising your arms straight up behind you, keeping your hands clasped. Exhale and slowly bend forward, keeping your hands clasped. Touch the floor with your forehead and hold for several seconds. Come back to starting position and relax. Repeat several times.

POSTURE # 14 - Child Pose

Sit on your heels. Lengthen the abdomen, bend forward and rest the abdomen on the thighs. Place your head on the floor or touching your knees. Rest the arms loosely at the sides. Deep breathe and relax for fifteen or twenty seconds. This posture can be a relaxing and rest position whenever you feel tired or tense or after an exercise session. It stretches all the muscles in the back and releases pain, strain and tension in the feet.

POSTURE # 15 - Head Rotations

Sit comfortable on the floor. Inhale. Now exhale as you slowly bring your head down close to your chest in a comfortable position. You will notice a gentle stretch on the back of your neck and shoulders. Now bring the head back to the center and relax. Inhale as you slowly roll your right ear towards your right shoulder. Without any quick or jerky movements, bring your shoulder up to your ear. Inhale as you continue to rotate your head past your right shoulder and drop your head gently backwards. Relax your jaw as you roll your head around to your left shoulder as you exhale. Continue around to the beginning position. Repeat movements several times in each direction.

POSTURE # 16 - Shoulder Shrugs

Stand or sit in a comfortable position with arms loosely hanging by your sides. Push both shoulders forward. Slowly raise them towards your ears. As your shoulders continue to rise, let them rotate back towards your ears. At the top of the rotation, gently push the shoulders back as you lower them to the starting position. Make a complete circle with each shoulder. Do this two or three times. Now rotate the shoulders in the opposite direction. Each shoulder can be rotated individually.

This posture can be done sitting down or standing. It is an excellent movement after you have been sitting at the wheel of your automobile during a long drive.

CHAPTER FOUR - RELAXATION-BREATHING-
VISUALIZATION

Stress is a major contributor to heart disease. When folks are under stress, more free radicals are formed, which cause a greater conversion of normal cholesterol into oxidized cholesterol (oxysterols). These oxysterols then build up in white blood cells and are carried to the site of damage in the arteries. Stress also stimulates the release of adrenalin, which in turn has been shown to cause platelet aggregation (blood clotting) and increased blood viscosity. Increases in blood viscosity can result in spontaneous clot formation. These can either adhere to arterial walls, initiating further plaque formation, or become lodged in narrowed arteries or capillaries, initiating a heart attack or stroke.

Decreasing stress in our life should be primary. Yoga has been especially beneficial for me in controlling stress. Yoga offers an excellent method to slow down the mind and body, thereby, relieving the body from stress. With daily periods spent practicing various postures, you will have one of the best tools known to man to keep your body well tuned and functioning as it was meant to be when you were born.

Cholesterol production is caused by chronic stress. A change in lifestyle (avoiding stress-inducing situations) will result in stress reduction that will decrease cholesterol production.

We must make a change in the way we perceive external situations. Learn not to be bothered by some of the things that now get under your skin.

In order to manage stress, we must change how we react to a situation. The circumstances don't change, but you do. A good example, especially for me, is driving in congested traffic. This can be very exasperating at times. My solution is; be a courteous driver, give the right-of-way to the other driver, leave fifteen minutes early and drive carefully.

Waiting in long lines can cause stress to some people. Such stressful situations can be handled in different ways. I learned a unique approach recently while standing in a long line at the grocery store. A few people were anxious for the line to move faster and became agitated. Their body action and the expression on their faces told the whole story. Observing these people was an elderly gentlemen standing next to me. He said;

"Waiting in line is part of life. It is expected in large communities. I have spent a good part of my life standing in line. It doesn't bother me now as it did in my younger years. I consider this a good time to 'pray'. It brings peace to my mind, and before I know it, I'm through the line."

What a great lesson! I have put this into my stress management program. Waiting in long lines is not a problem.

Also, I practice deep (abdominal) breathing while driving, a practice I learned through yoga. Deep breathing relaxes and calms the nerves and allows you to remain cool-headed in stressful situations.

Relaxation and abdominal breathing is considered, in my opinion, the most enjoyable part of yoga. Together with visualization, it is an essential phase of reversing heart disease.

Relaxation -   Let's start with relaxing your muscles. Your muscles will relax more profoundly if they are first tensed. Take a position on your back. Close your eyes. Get into a comfortable position and then try to lie without moving. Inhale and tense your right leg. Raise it a few inches off the floor and hold it there for a few seconds. Now let it drop to the floor as you exhale. Repeat with your left leg.

Now inhale deeply and contract the muscles of the right arm as you raise it a few inches off the floor. Hold it there for about four to six seconds, and then let it drop to the floor while you exhale. Repeat with the left arm.

Inhale deeply and push your abdomen outward, holding your breath for about five seconds while contracting your abdomen. Now let your abdomen completely relax as you exhale through your mouth. Repeat in the same manner with your chest.

Let your arms relax.   Now inhale and bring your shoulders up toward your ears, then bring them together in front of your chest, and then push them toward your feet. Now relax.

Finally, slowly roll your head from side to side and let your neck relax.

Abdominal Breathing - You have now relaxed your body with the above exercises and should be ready for abdominal breathing exercises.   Abdominal breathing assists the flow of oxygen into the bloodstream and reduces stress.   Inhaled oxygen, transferred from the lungs into the bloodstream, is one of the body's basic fuels. We use this deep breathing method as a form of stress reduction, relaxation and pain reduction.

When you observe the breathing of a newborn baby, they breathe first in the belly, then they lift the diaphragm and then the chest and the clavicle. This is the way we should breathe as we grow. But it doesn't happen. As we age and take on more responsibilities we become stressed out at an early age. Our breathing becomes short and shallow and causes the rib cage to get tighter and tighter resulting in lighter breaths throughout our day. When this happens, we are using only the upper portion of the lungs for shallow breathing. In abdominal (deep) breathing, using the lower portion of the lungs is a more effective way of getting oxygen into the blood.

Begin with Posture # 17 - Abdominal Breathing.

POSTURE # 17 - *Abdominal Breathing*
Sit comfortable. Exhale slowly and smoothly and contract your abdominal muscles. As you exhale, the stomach moves inward. Now relax your abdomen and

slowly and smoothly inhale. The stomach moves outward as you inhale, pushing your abdominal muscles forward slightly arching your lower back. Now exhale. When you contract your abdominal muscles, the stomach will move inward and will flatten your back. Repeat this movement several times as you breathe smoothly and steadily through your nose.

Place your right hand on your chest and your left hand on your abdomen. Inhale. If your right hand rises more than your left hand, then you are breathing from your chest. If your left hand rises more than your right hand, then you are breathing from your diaphragm

Majority of people breathe from their chest, which is usually rapid, shallow, and irregular. This type of breathing is known as the fight-or-flight response which can create stressful feelings associated with that response.

If you are experiencing difficulty learning how to breathe from your abdomen, then lie on the floor in the resting position and place a small object on you abdomen. Abdominal breathing will cause the object to rise and fall as you inhale and exhale.

Now assume a sitting position and relax your muscles. For breath awareness focus your attention to your breathing. As you inhale and exhale, visualize the flow of your breath entering through your nostrils, down to your abdomen and then as it returns outward as you exhale. Your breathing should be natural, deep, smooth, rhythmic, and diaphragmatic. Also, it should be silent without pauses or holding the breath. Mentally visualize this breathing action.

The length of inhaling should be equal with the length of exhalation and you should not hold your breath or have pauses between inhalation and exhalation. Also, be aware of your stomach moving in and out, and the air entering and leaving your nostrils. Practice your deep breathing and breath awareness exercises for several times daily, approximately ten to fifteen minutes each exercise period. Following a month of daily periods of breath awareness, you should be able to prolong the exhalation twice the length of inhalation.

Since learning abdominal breathing and practicing breath awareness, I have used it in many situations that have helped me relax and to avoid being stressed out. Concentrate on deep abdominal breathing and it will calm the nerves. You can also practice deep breathing on long trips, whether you are driving are flying. In fact, deep breathing can be done anytime and anywhere.

Alternate Nostril Breathing - Yoga teaches us that the rhythm of alternate-nostril breathing is important in maintaining physiological and psychological equilibrium. Our noses are lined with erectile tissue that expands and contracts during the day. This causes our nasal mucosa to swell and shrink.

The flow of air through our nose shifts from one nostril to the other during the day as the lining of each nostril expands and contracts in a biological rhythm. The breath normally flows predominantly through one nostril for about two hours, and then the predominance will begin to shift to the other nostril.

Alternate nostril breathing was developed to rebalance the equilibrium of breathing and is a powerful tool for calming and relaxing the mind and body. Begin with Posture # 18 - Alternate Nostril Breathing.

POSTURE # 18 - *Alternate Nostril Breathing*
Sit on the floor in a still and steady position. Close your eyes and concentrate on relaxing your muscles and calm your body. Exhale deeply through both nostrils. Now, close off your right nostril with your thumb and inhale slowly through your left nostril. Press your ring finger against your left nostril, removing your thumb from your

right nostril and slowly exhale through the right nostril. After exhaling through right nostril, keep the left nostril closed and inhale. Now close off the right and exhale through the left. Continue this pattern and when you become comfortable with the breathing technique, gradually increase the exhalations until they are about twice as long as the inhalations.

Visualization - A very important phase in using yoga to reverse heart disease is the visualization period. Our body responds to images, good and bad. Close your eyes and visualize a happy moment. Maybe it was taking food to a sick friend. Visualize the smile that came across your friend's face and the appreciation that was expressed for such a kind act. It made you feel good. Now, pay attention to what happens to your body. Your body now becomes relaxed and your breathing is deeper and more regular, and your heart rate has slowed.

Do the opposite now. Think of a bad situation that caused you to be upset. Notice that your breathing has become more rapid and shallow, your muscles have tightened. Your heart rate is much faster and you feel angry and disturbed.

I suppose one of the best examples of visualization (also known as imagery) and its effect on our body, can be illustrated by our dreams, especially with nightmares. Do you remember awaking in the middle of the night with your body covered with sweat? Your heart is pounding like a base drum and your muscles are all tensed up. All of this was created by images from the mind during the period of dreaming. Boy, that nightmare really stressed you out!

Let's use this imagery to reverse your hear disease. Here is the imagery I have used since July 1993. Using one of the illustrations of my Coronary Artery Diagrams, I visualize the diagram, or the image of my heart, and focus on a source of white energy flowing rapidly through my arteries and dissolving all of the congested areas and opening up all blockages. Here is the posture that I get into:

POSTURE # 19 - *Visualization or Imagery*
Sit on the floor in an upright position with legs crossed. Grasp hands behind your back with eyes closed. Inhale deeply. Now exhale as you lower your head toward your abdomen. Keep your head bowed in a comfortable position and breathe normally. Create an image of your heart. Become aware of your breathing. Imagine that each time you exhale a great force of energy rushes through your arteries flowing into your heart and energizing your entire body.

I always precede my image with a prayer, asking my Lord to help my body to manufacture healthy blood that will rush through my arteries like a source of white energy, dissolving all congested areas.

CHAPTER FIVE - HERBS-VITAMINS-MINERALS-NATURAL FOOD SUPPLEMENTS

"And God said, behold I have given you every herb bearing seed, which is upon the face of all the earth, and every tree, in the which is the fruit of a tree yielding seed; to you it shall be for food." Genesis 1:29.

Herbs are intended for our use. The bible refers to herbs more than 3000 times.

Look to nature and allow what God has provided for man to heal himself and to be his own doctor through the use of nature's herbs. This natural method is simpler, more natural, less stressful, creates a more personal responsibility for learning to care for our health and practicing self-care, and to live in line with nature rather than the demands of corporations and other vested interests that work against our health.

Remedial properties of herbs and the juices of fruits and vegetables have been recognized and appreciated since Adam and Eve. During the sixteenth century, medicines were artificially prepared from chemicals. Modern medicine now makes us more and more dependent on synthetic drugs which poisons our bodies and causes bad aftereffects.

Drug manufacturers cannot patent natural substances . Large profits come from synthetic and unnatural substances that they patent allowing for huge profits. Our government has designed and built a profit system that mediates against the natural state of health. Synthetic drugs do not fit accurately into our molecular system. These synthetics produce side effects because of this "non-compatible" relationship with nature creating disease conditions caused by poisoning from toxic properties in the molecular makeup of these unnatural substances.

We believe the healing properties of herbs are just as effective as drugs, but without the side effects. Plants produce a wide range of vitamins and hundreds of natural antioxidants. If we would only teach our children the healing virtues of plants and what great values that are enhanced in natural foods, half of the sickness and deaths in early life would be unknown.

There is a herb for every disease that attacks the human body. Research has proven that herbs are beneficial in reversing heart disease.

We have researched herbs, vitamins, minerals and natural food supplements that are beneficial in reversing heart disease and will discuss them in this chapter.

-GARLIC-

Garlic is one of the most valuable foods on earth and has been used since ancient times of the Hebrews, Greeks, Babylonians, Romans and Egyptians. Pyramid builders ate garlic daily for endurance and strength.

Garlic is useful in orchestrating and blocking atherosclerosis and in reducing blood cholesterol. It has been known to lower serum cholesterol and triglycerides, while also raising HDL (good) levels in both healthy individuals and patients of coronary heart disease. Garlic helps protect against narrowing of the arteries and is known to dissolve LDL (bad) cholesterol and to lower triglycerides, while increasing HDL cholesterol.

The chemical and nutrient contents of garlic are: unsaturated aldehydes, allicin, allyl disulfides, calcium, copper, germanium, iron, magnesium, manganese, volatile oils, phosphorus, phytoncides, potassium, selenium, sulfur, vitamins A, B, B2 and C and zinc.

Garlic is a natural antibiotic and is so effective that one milligram of allicin (its major component) is about equal to fifteen standard units of penicillin. Garlic protects from infection, detoxifies the body, strengthens blood vessels and lowers blood pressure. It aids in the treatment of arteriosclerosis, asthma, arthritis, cancer, circulatory problems, colds, flu, digestive problems, heart disorders, insomnia, liver disease, sinusitis, ulcers and yeast infections.

Garlic can target infections just about anywhere in the body because its potent oils are readily absorbed and transported throughout the body. The absorption rate of oil or juice from garlic is so powerful that when applied to the soles of the feet, will pass through the body to the lungs so rapidly that it can be detected on the breath within seconds.

-HAWTHORN-

Hawthorn improves coronary circulation by dilating the coronary arteries and relieving spasms of the arterial walls.

Hawthorn is an excellent preventative prescription for individuals who have a family history of heart disease. It is a safe and effective long-term treatment for the gradual loss of heart function that comes with age. Hawthorn is not habit forming or toxic and is most effective when used in conjunction with a healthy diet and exercise program. It speeds recovery of heart patients, strengthens the heart and wards off coronary disease. Hawthorn has the ability to increase oxygen utilization by the heart, it increases enzyme metabolism in the heart muscle, it acts as a very mild dilator of coronary vessels. It also dilates the blood vessels away from the heart, thus, lowering the blood pressure and reduces the burden placed on the heart.

As a cardiac tonic, it is valuable for improvement of cardiac weakness, valve murmurs from heart valve defects, an enlarged heart, angina, sighing respiration and chronic fatigue. Hawthorn has shown to be effective in easing cardiac pain, regulating rapid or feeble heart beat.

Hawthorn increases coronary blood flow and improves myocardial metabolism allowing the heart to function with less oxygen. This effective herb dilates blood vessels, allowing blood to flow more freely. It also acts directly on the heart muscle to help a damaged heart function more efficiently. No other herb provides the nourishing regeneration of Hawthorn both before or after a heart attack.

For optimum effect, I take the *extract* capsules.

-CAYENNE-

Cayenne is one of the most effective stimulants that targets the digestive and the circulatory system primarily. Cayenne strengthens the pulse, feeds the heart, regulates blood pressure, thins the blood, lowers cholesterol, cleanses the circulatory system, stops hemorrhaging, speeds healing of wounds, heals ulcers, rebuilds damaged tissue, aids digestion, eases congestion, relieves arthritis and rheumatism, regulates elimination, numbs pain and prevents the spread of infection.

Cayenne influences the flow of digestive secretions from salivary, gastric and intestinal glands. It will increase thermogenesis for weight loss and gives the system a cardiovascular lift by exciting the heart; thus, effectively increasing circulation.

Excellent for warding off diseases and equalizing blood circulation, Cayenne works to prevent strokes and heart attacks. It is useful to arrest hemorrhaging (external and internal) and it is cleansing and healing when used to purify external wounds. Cayenne increases the heart action without increasing the blood pressure and improves the ratio of HDL cholesterol.

Your circulatory system benefits from the use of Cayenne by helping the arteries, veins and capillaries regain the elasticity of youth by feeding the cell structure. The circulation is equalized by regulating the flow of blood from head to feet. Cayenne strengthens the pulse by increasing the power.

Cayenne helps prevent the build-up of cholesterol which can narrow the veins and arteries; plus, it helps thin the blood and prevent blood clots that can clog the arteries and cause stroke and heart attack. Studies have shown that Cayenne stimulates the body's fibrinolytic system helping prevent clots from forming and dissolving clots that had already formed.

-GINKGO BILOBA-

Ginkgo Biloba has been shown to protect the body from arterial blockages. Various other uses have been as an aid in the treatment of problems associated with aging, such as poor blood circulation, mental confusion, memory loss and many of the disruptions expected with the onset of senility. Significant increase in mental alertness and memory has been credited to the use of Ginkgo.

Ginkgo inhibits free radical scavengers from destroying cells. The elixir in Ginkgo has been found to be effective in reducing blood cell clumping. Clumping of blood can bring on congestive heart disease. The increase in acetyl-choline levels from the use of Ginkgo allows the body to better transmit body electrical impulses. Ginkgo also improves blood circulation to the central nervous system, aids in the treatment of dementia, Alzheimer's disease and Meniere's Syndrome.

There is a strong possibility of preventing strokes when Ginkgo strengthens the blood vascular system and decreases the possibilities of clots. It also dilates the blood vessels, facilitating improved blood flow to the tissues. For patients recovering from blood clots in the arteries of the heart, Ginkgo has been found to lower blood pressure and dilate peripheral blood vessels, including the capillaries.

-GOTU KOLA-

Gotu Kola is considered to be one of the best herbal nerve tonics. It improves the learning ability by facilitating better recall. Also, it acts as a cleanser of the blood, therefore, it strengthens the heart and balances the hormones and the nervous system and improves blood circulation. The herb is known for its calming effect.

Known for its value as a nervous system restorative, Gotu Kola has also been found to exhibit wound-healing capabilities. It increases mental activity while acting as a mild tranquilizer and combats fatigue and is also used to improve memory and is a blood cleanser for skin disease.

High blood pressure can be treated with Gotu Kola and it is also effective as a treatment for mental problems dealing with anxiety and loss of memory. Gotu Kola is often referred to as the memory herb because it is known to stimulate circulation to the brain.

-GINGER-

Ginger has been shown to lower cholesterol levels and make the blood platelets less sticky. Research has found that Ginger may help prevent strokes and hardening of the arteries. Gingerol, the active ingredient of Ginger, has been proven to be effective in preventing recurrences of mild strokes. Gingerol is believed to inhibit an enzyme that causes cells to clot.

Many doctors prescribe Aspirin for their heart patients for the blood thinning properties which help prevent heart problems. The fact is Aspirin has serious side effects such as causing stomach and intestinal ulcers, which often hemorrhage causing death. Aspirin also blocks Ginger's action to prevent blood platelets from clumping. Aspirin can prevent the clotting that prevents strokes, however, it also prevents Ginger from naturally doing a better job of preventing harmful problems.

Ginger is a body cleansing and warm blood vascular stimulant herb. It is used in respiratory and lung/chest clearing combinations, plus, it is a system alkalizer and a stimulant of the digestive system.

Ginger has long been recommended by herbalist as a regulator of blood cholesterol to improve blood circulation, especially to the hands and feet.

Most effective, Ginger prevents nausea caused by motion sickness. From a personal point of view, Ginger has been a "Godsend" for my wife Joy. Suffering from Meniere's Disease (recurrent attacks of dizziness) since 1978, Ginger has been her choice of preventing nausea by taking one capsule prior to traveling. There are no side effects with the use of Ginger.

-VALERIAN ROOT-

Valerian root slows the action of the heart while increasing its general force. It has been used for centuries to calm many forms of nervous disorders. It produces a putrid odor akin to that of bad cheese or mildewed clothing, however, Valerian soothes the nerves, quietens heart palpitations, stimulates digestion, strengthens the circulatory system, heals ulcers, relieves anxiety, eases hypertension and calms hyperactivity.

A primary sedative, Valerian is used when sleep disorders are the result of anxiety, nervousness, exhaustion, headache or hysteria. It has an influence on the cerebrospinal system and is used as a sedative of the primary nerve centers for afflictions such as St. Vitus Dance (Chorea), nervous unrest, neuralgia pain, epileptic seizures, hysteria, restlessness and wakefulness.

Valerian is suggested for cases of heart palpitation, because it slows down the heart rate while increasing the strength of the beats. It is one of the best herbal sources of calcium and magnesium. This herb is anti-spasmodic and equalizing, therefore, it acts as a sedative in states of agitation and a stimulant in fatigue. It has long been used as a stomachic, anti-spasmodic, carminative and antidote to the plague. Since ancient times, has been used in the treatment of epilepsy. Valerian's best known use is as a natural tranquilizer.

-COENZYME Q10-

Coenzyme Q10 (CoQ10) has been recognized as one of the most exciting nutrient discoveries in recent decades. CoQ10's essential role as a coenzyme in the production of energy is just the tip of the ice berg of the benefits this remarkable nutrient provides.

Studies have shown CoQ10 to be effective in lowering blood pressure, enhancing the immune system, strengthening the heart and protecting against periodontal disease. It is an antioxidant with all the attending benefits, plus it has been useful to people with AIDS, cancer, diabetes and chronic fatigue syndrome.

The primary function of CoQ10 is as a catalyst to the creation of energy on a cellular level. Each of our cells contains tiny energy generators called mitochondria. The mitochondria produce ninety-five percent of our total energy needs. Adenosine triphosphate (ATP) is the basic energy molecule of the cell. CoQ10 must be present for the syntheses of ATP.

Studies have shown that if levels of CoQ10 decline by twenty-five percent, our organs and systems will not have the energy they need to function correctly. Major ill health and disease states are the result. A seventy-five percent deficiency is fatal. On the other hand, using CoQ10 to correct a deficiency state has an overall rejuvenating effect on the body.

CoQ10 is the last of a series of coenzymes of the "Q" type. The "10" refers to the length of its "tail." CoQs of varying lengths are found everywhere in life and in most of the foods we eat. CoQ10 has been called "ubiquinone" because of its ubiquitous presence. For most of our lives our livers are able to take any of the CoQs and synthesize the CoQ10 we need. Between the age of thirty-five and forty, our ability to synthesize CoQ10 begins to decline. This is also the age when many people begin to experience a decrease in energy and a general deterioration of their health.

More CoQ10 is found in the heart tissue than in any other muscle of the body. This is also the most prolific area of scientific research with CoQ10. It has been associated with the treatment of heart attack, valvular heart disease, coronary artery thrombosis, angina and high blood pressure (a high risk factor for heart disease).

Dr. Karl Folkers, University of Texas, is recognized as the father of CoQ research in the U.S. He compared blood samples from one hundred patients suffering from CHD (coronary heart disease) with a healthy control group. The CoQ levels for the cardiac sufferers were a significant twenty-five percent less than those of the healthier subjects. In summation, Dr. Folkers has found CoQ10 to be deficient in the heart tissue of about seventy-five percent of all CHD sufferers. The good news is that therapeutic effects have been reported by about seventy percent of those using CoQ10 as a dietary supplement.

Dr. Folkers concludes that it is not heart disease that results in a CoQ10 deficiency but that in about 70 percent of cases, it is the deficiency that results in heart disease.

The American Journal of Cardiology reported in 1985 the therapeutic benefits of CoQ10 in the treatment of angina pectoris. This form of heart disease is caused by constricted arteries. The narrowed arteries are not able to deliver the additional oxygen needed by the heart muscle during emotional excitement or exercise. The pain of an attack is immobilizing and terrifying. First time sufferers frequently have the additional anguish believing that they are having a heart attack. When angina sufferers were given CoQ10 supplementation, the incidence of attacks was halved after only four weeks as was the need for nitroglycerin tablets.

-LECITHIN-

Lecithin is needed by every living cell in the human body. Cell membranes, which regulate which nutrients may leave or enter the cell, are largely composed of lecithin. Without lecithin, the cell membranes would harden. Its structure protects the cells from damage by oxidation. The protective sheaths surrounding the brain are composed of lecithin, and the muscles and nerve cells also contain this essential fatty substance. Lecithin, which is largely composed of the B vitamin choline, also contains linoleic acid and inositol. Although lecithin is a fatty substance, it acts as an emulsifying agent.

It is especially important that the elderly obtain this nutrient because it helps prevent arteriosclerosis, protects against cardiovascular disease, increases brain function and aids in the absorption of thiamine by the liver and vitamin A by the intestine. Lecithin is also known to promote energy and is needed to help repair the damage to the liver caused by alcoholism.

Lecithin is a wise addition to your diet. I use one to two tablespoons of lecithin granules on my cereal every morning - it's delicious. It can be added to soups, juices and breads. Lecithin also comes in capsule form. Taking one capsule before meals helps the digestion of fats and absorption of the fat-soluble vitamins. Those taking niacin for high serum cholesterol and triglycerides need to include lecithin in their diet. Lecithin enables fats, such as cholesterol and other lipids, to be dispersed in water and removed from the body. The vital organs and arteries are protected from fatty build-up with the inclusion of lecithin in the diet.

-L-CARNITINE-

L-Carnitine helps to transport long-chain fatty acids. By preventing fatty build-up, this amino acid aids in weight loss, decreases the risk for heart disease, and improves athletic ability. Carnitine can be manufactured in the body if sufficient amounts of lysine, BI, B6 and iron are available. Vegetarians are more likely to be deficient in carnitine due to a diet that is low in lysine.

Carnitine also enhances the effectiveness of antioxidant vitamins E and C.

-VITAMIN C-

The lack of vitamin C in the body subjects the inner lining of the arteries to damage. Stress can destroy this vital ingredient in the body. Small tears can occur in the lining of the arteries after a sudden very high blood pressure episode brought on by stress. If sufficient antioxidants are present in the bloodstream (vitamin C, vitamin E and beta-carotene) oxysterols (oxidized cholesterol) can be neutralized and prevented from damaging the vessel walls. However, stress depletes the body of vitamin C, and this depletion can lead to a further buildup of homocysteine, which can in turn cause the generation of oxysterols.

Studies have shown that vitamin C supplementation can reverse arteriosclerosis in humans. Vitamin C prevents free radical formation.

In a diet that involves reducing fats, vitamin C is an integral part of helping the body to repair itself.

Studies have shown that the U.S. Recommended Daily Allowance (RDA) of vitamin C offered virtually no protection against arterial damage. Researchers have found that a dose equivalent to 2,800 milligrams for a one hundred and fifty pound person, reversed the damage.

Some doctors recommend that vitamin C be taken to bowel tolerance (the maximum amount you can take before causing diarrhea). They suggest a minimum of three to four doses daily, increasing the amount until reaching bowel tolerance. Such as, the first dose could be one thousand milligrams, the second dose two, the third three and the fourth four thousand milligrams. Maintain this bowel tolerance until cardiovascular disease is resolved, then go on three thousand milligrams maintenance dose.

Vitamin C is an antioxidant that is required for tissue growth and repair, adrenal gland function, and healthy gums. It protects against the harmful effects of pollution, prevents cancer, protects against infection and enhances immunity. It also may reduce cholesterol levels and high blood pressure, and prevent atherosclerosis.

-VITAMIN B6-

Researchers have found that vitamin B6 may be helpful in preventing heart attacks and strokes. It is also believed to inhibit the platelet aggregation which occurs in atherosclerosis.

In 1969, interest in vitamin B6 deficiency and its relationship to heart disease was revived, when Kilmer S. McCully, M.D., a Professor of Pathology at Harvard Medical School, found that heart patients had nearly eighty percent less of the vitamin than healthy individuals. From this study, Dr. McCully assumed that B6 may help the body resist the arterial damage that precipitates heart disease. Also, it was found that patients who had already suffered a heart attack or angina, and were then given two hundred milligrams of B6 daily (half in a B complex including choline), combined with a low-fat, mostly vegetarian diet, recovered rapidly.

-VITAMIN B12-
Vitamin B12 is needed to prevent anemia. It benefits cell formation and cellular longevity. Other needs for this vitamin is for proper digestion, absorption of foods, protein synthesis, and metabolism of carbohydrates and fats. Also, vitamin B12 prevents nerve damage, maintains fertility and promotes normal growth and development. A deficiency of this vitamin can be caused by malabsorption, which is most common in the elderly and in those with digestive disorders. Vegetarians are also more likely to have a B12 deficiency. Abnormal gait, memory loss, hallucinations, eye disorders, anemia, and digestive disorders are symptoms of B12 deficiency.
Vegetarians need a vitamin B12 supplement because this vitamin is found mostly in animal sources.

-VITAMIN E-
Vitamin E is an antioxidant that prevents cancer and cardiovascular disease. This supplement improves circulation, repairs tissue, promotes normal clotting and

healing, reduces scarring from some wounds, reduces blood pressure, aids in preventing cataracts and aids leg cramps. Vitamin E also prevents formation of free radicals, retards aging and may prevent age spots as well.

Supplementation of vitamin E may also inhibit platelet aggregation and help repair lining cells of blood vessels.

Studies published in *The New England Journal of Medicine* suggest that vitamin E can contribute greatly to the prevention of heart disease in both men and women. In one study done at Harvard Medical School, involving a group of 87,245 female nurses, it was found that those who took one hundred International Units of vitamin E daily for more than two years had a forty-six percent lower risk of heart disease. In another study, 39,910 male health professionals who took one hundred IU of vitamin E daily for an unspecified time period had a thirty-seven percent lower risk of heart disease. Groups who took higher doses of vitamin E for a longer time produced even greater results.

It was shown in another study among sixteen European study populations, those with low serum levels of vitamin E were at greater risk for heart disease than those with high blood pressure and high cholesterol levels.

-FOLIC ACID-

Studies have shown that folic acid can dramatically lower homocysteine, a free radical generator capable of oxidizing cholesterol, one of the major contributing factors in heart disease. Folic acid is essential for the proper metabolism of homocysteine.

Folic acid is considered a brain food and is needed for energy production and the formation of red blood cells.

Functioning as a coenzyme in DNA synthesis, it is important for healthy cell division and replication. Folic acid helps in protein metabolism and may help depression and anxiety and may be effective in the treatment of uterine cervical dysplasia. It is essential in regulating embryonic and fetal development of nerve cells, vital for normal growth and development.

Greater results are experienced when folic acid is combined with vitamin B12. One sign of a deficiency in folic acid is a sore, red tongue.

-CHROMIUM PICOLINALE-

Chromium supplementation has been shown to lower total cholesterol and triglycerides and raise HDL cholesterol. It is even more effective in lowering cholesterol when combined with niacin (vitamin B3). Studies have shown that a chromium deficiency has been linked to coronary heart disease.

-MAGNESIUM-

Studies show that individuals who die suddenly of heart attacks have far lower levels of magnesium and potassium than control groups. Magnesium helps to dilate arteries and ease the heart's pumping of blood, therefore preventing arrhythmias (irregular heartbeats). Magnesium may also prevent calcification of the blood vessels, lower total cholesterol, raise HDL cholesterol, and inhibit platelet aggregation.

Magnesium is vital to enzyme activity. It assists in calcium and potassium uptake. Supplementing the diet with magnesium helps prevent depression, dizziness, muscle weakness, twitching, heart disease and high blood pressure and also aids in maintaining the proper pH balance. This essential mineral protects the arterial lining from stress caused by sudden blood pressure changes, and plays a role in the formation of bone and in carbohydrate and mineral metabolism.

For optimum absorption and effectiveness, use magnesium glycinate, taurate, or aspartate, or even herbal magnesium such as red raspberry.

-FREE RADICALS-

The free radical is a chemical invader that has the ability to penetrate a cell and cause changes in the DNA, producing mutation.

Free radicals, in small numbers, are normally present in our body. Biochemical processes naturally lead to the formation of these critters, and under normal conditions our body can keep them at bay. When our body is exposed to ionizing radiation, this activates the free radical formation; therefore, the formation of a large number of free radicals stimulates the formation of more of these demon like critters leading to greater instability.

Free radicals can cause a lot of damage. It could cause changes in the cells that make up muscular layers found in the arteries where cardiovascular disease begins.

Cooking fats at high temperatures, particularly frying foods in oil, can produce high numbers of free radicals. We get free radicals from; consumption of unsaturated oils (especially rancid oils), meats, alcohol, smoking, radiation, chlorinated water, constipation and toxic chemicals.

Supplementing the diet with antioxidants (herbs and vitamins A, C and E) will help to detoxify our body and prevent the formation of free radicals.

The following is a list of the natural sources for various vitamins and minerals:

Vitamin C Natural Sources: Green vegetables, berries, citrus fruits, asparagus, beet greens, broccoli, Brussels sprouts, cantaloupe, collards, currants, grapefruit, kale, lemons, mangos, mustard greens, onions, oranges, papayas, parsley, green peas, sweet peppers, persimmons, pineapple, radishes, rose hips, spinach, strawberries, Swiss chard, tomatoes, turnip greens and watercress.

Vitamin A (Beta-Carotene) Natural Sources: Sweet potatoes, broccoli, carrots, Swiss chard, garlic, kale, mustard, parsley, peaches, red peppers, spinach, blue-green algae, pumpkins, turnip greens, watercress, mango and cantaloupe.

Vitamin E Natural Sources: Cold-pressed vegetable oils, whole grains, dark green leafy vegetables (in cabbage, vitamin E is richest in the outer leaves, which are often removed), nuts, seeds, legumes, dry beans, brown rice, cornmeal, eggs, milk, oatmeal, sweet potatoes, soybeans, all bean sprouts, asparagus, cucumber and wheat germ.

Vitamin B1 Natural Sources: Dried beans, brown rice, fish, peanuts, peas, poultry, soybeans, whole grains, broccoli, Brussels sprouts, most nuts, oat meal, plums, dried prunes and raisins.

Vitamin B2 Natural Sources: Beans, cheese, eggs, fish, milk, spinach, poultry, yogurt, broccoli, Brussels sprouts and nuts.

Vitamin B3 Natural Sources: Broccoli, carrots, cheese, corn flour, eggs, fish, milk, pork, potatoes, tomatoes and whole wheat.

Vitamin B6 Natural Sources: All foods contain small amounts of vitamin B6, however, the following foods have the highest amounts: Brewer's yeast, carrots, eggs, chicken, fish, peas, spinach, sunflower seeds, walnuts and wheat germ. Other sources not quite as rich include: bananas, beans, brown rice, cabbage, cantaloupes and other whole grains.

Vitamin B12 Natural Sources: Blue cheese, cheese, clams, eggs, milk, seafood, tofu, soy milk, herring, kidney, liver and mackerel.

Folic Acid Natural Sources: Barley, beans, beef, bran, brewer's yeast, brown rice, cheese, chicken, dates, green leafy vegetables, lamb, lentils, liver, milk, oranges, organ meats, split peas, pork, root vegetables, salmon, tuna, wheat germ, whole grains, whole wheat and yeast.

Chromium Picolinale Natural Sources: Brewer's yeast, brown rice, cheese, whole grains, dried beans, dairy products, mushrooms and potatoes.

Calcium Natural Sources: Salmon, green leafy vegetables, almonds, brewer's yeast, broccoli, buttermilk, cabbage, figs, kale, mustard, oats, parsley, prunes, sesame seeds, tofu, turnip greens, whey and yogurt.

Potassium Natural Sources: Bananas, brown rice, dates, figs, dried fruit, garlic, nuts, potatoes, raisins, yams, dairy foods, fish, fruit, legumes, vegetables and whole grains.

Magnesium Natural Sources: Magnesium is found in most foods, especially dairy products, fish, meat, and seafood. Other rich food sources include apples, apricots, avocados, bananas, blackstrap molasses, brewer's yeast, brown rice, figs, garlic, kelp, lima beans, millet, nuts, peaches, black-eyed peas, salmon, sesame seeds, tofu, tourla, green leafy vegetables, wheat and whole grains.

- The NOW brand is a good brand for herbs, vitamins and minerals.

CHAPTER SIX - RECIPES

There are no other vegetarians in our family. Both Joy and I came from a long line of meat eaters. Barbecue is a talent that was extended from both of our families. It was unheard of not to have a barbecue grill or pit in your back yard. I remember the aroma of sausage and spare ribs on the grill - chicken breasts and a one-inch thick club steak. Also, there were cheeseburgers and baked potatoes with lots of butter. Do I remember the taste? You betcha! Could I eat it now? Not likely, especially when I *know* what this sort of fat will do to my arteries. I am not interested in playing Russian roulette. Ask yourself - is it worth it? My answer to this question is a resounding NO!

Who in their right mind would want to go back to suffering from angina and taking Mevacor or Pravacor, Cardizem, wearing nitroglycerin patches, carrying a supply of nitroglycerin pills and wondering (if you lived through it all) when is the next surgery going to be? I'd have to have rocks in my head just to consider such a thing! Besides, I thoroughly enjoy the foods that we eat now. They are tasty, wholesome and just downright delicious.

Prior to my diet my weight topped out at one hundred and eighty pounds. My weight now is one hundred and fifty-five pounds and is in line with my height of five feet, ten and a half inches. This is what I weighed when discharged from the Navy in 1954. I could wear that old Navy uniform.

Joy has been with me on this diet every step of the way, even though she has never had a heart problem. However, prior to our vegetarian diet her cholesterol level was high, causing us much concern. She lost twenty-five pounds and dropped her cholesterol sixty points. Joy is a profound believer in our diet and has never been healthier. Our good health keeps her motivated in the kitchen. We would never go back to eating unhealthy foods again.

I am not the cook in our family. Joy does all of the cooking and I just sit back and reap the benefits. I will, on occasion, make a green salad or prepare veggie hamburgers or veggie hot dogs. Leftovers? Now this is a real snap and I can handle with no problem. Joy assigns K.P. duty for me. There are no complaints here. If she does the cooking, I will gladly clean up afterwards. I learned many years ago the worst thing (in regards to cooking) a person can do is upset the cook. This is an absolute no-no!

The recipes listed in this chapter are the vegetables we like, however, you may add or exchange any to your liking.

Eating better means living better. Spending time in the kitchen is a small price to pay for good health and an extended (good) life.

The transition to a vegetarian-oriented, whole foods diet may seem daunting, however, this change may be easier and more pleasurable than imagined and considering the enormous health benefits, is worth it. As a vegetarian, there is no limit as to how much you can eat.

Joy cooks only once a day, but on occasions will cook twice. We both love our cold cereal with fresh fruit for breakfast, therefore, no cooking is required for the morning meal. The breakfast foods in the recipes are prepared for an evening meal on occasions.

Cooking is either at noon or in the afternoon. For one or the other meals, we have leftovers or very simple meals (veggie burgers, taquitos or bean sandwiches).

If you are tired or don't have much time, you can always throw some fresh veggies in the steamer, open up a can of beans or peas, put on a pan of corn bread and sit down to eat thirty minutes later. Pretty easy! Fresh fruit is the perfect dessert.

Occasionally, we treat ourselves with a lunch or dinner at a restaurant with a nice salad bar with non-fat dressing and a baked potato with steamed broccoli. We also go to Chinese restaurants and have steamed veggies with steamed rice. Most Italian restaurants make a minestrone soup that has no added fat. Take your own fat-free salad dressing and ask for bread sticks without butter.

Make yourself a week's planned menu every week.

For A Healthy Heart:

1. Be a vegetarian.
2. Strive to eat organic whole, nutrient and fiber-rich food.
3. Avoid refined, processed , preserved, packaged products.
4. If you eat dairy products, limit them to yogurt, cottage cheese (non-fat or low-fat 1%).
5. Never eat margarine, shortening or hydrogenated oils.
6. Exercise daily.

The possibilities that vegetarian cooking offer are endless. We hope these recipes will inspire you to cook with a new outlook on food. Joy and I have a deep satisfaction knowing that we are eating healthy.

I reversed my heart disease in two years by abstaining from eating processed, refined foods and products containing hydrogenated oils. I ate the foods that Joy prepared for me from the recipes listed in this section. Combined with yoga, daily exercise and nutritional supplements (garlic, ginger, ginkgo, hawthorn, CoQ10, lecithin, red raspberry-magnesium, vitamin C, E, B-6 and B-12), this low-fat vegetarian diet did the trick.

You also, could have the same results. Life will be better for you. Circulatory problems yield quickly to diet and lifestyle modifications. With a diet based on whole grains and vegetables in conjunction with daily exercise, nearly everyone can expect significant vascular renewal within a few weeks. The *Journal of the American Medical Association* reports that most heart bypass operations would be unnecessary with as few as thirty days of a high-fiber, low-fat diet. My doctor told me, "If everyone followed your program I would be out of business."

Now, if you are really serious about good health, you must clean out your refrigerator and pantry. Get rid of everything that has fat in it, especially margarine and products with hydrogenated oil.

Begin with the Fourteen Day Menu Schedule. Develop a good healthy eating and daily exercise habit and stick with it. The more you adhere to your program, the more benefits you will receive.

Remember, it is not what you eat once in a while that builds your optimal body but what you eat most of the time.

FOURTEEN DAY MENU SCHEDULE

Breakfast is listed for first day only. You can substitute with your own choice for remaining schedule.

Day one:

Breakfast:
Shredded Wheat cereal
one tablespoon of lecithin granules
one tablespoon of ground flax seeds
one tablespoon raisins
blueberries
one banana
low-fat or non-fat Westsoy *vanilla soymilk*
If you must sweeten, use honey.

Noon Meal:
Corn soup
fresh baked whole wheat bread

Evening Meal:
Fettuccine with sun dried tomatoes
garlic bread
green salad

Day two:

Noon Meal:
Fat-free Veggie burgers
(Yves, Lightlife, Morningstar Farms)
oven fries
banana cake

-RECIPES-

Evening Meal:
*Hardy bean soup
green salad
fresh baked whole wheat bread*

Day three:

Noon Meal:
*Leftover soup
bread
fresh fruit*

Evening Meal:
*Pinto beans
steamed broccoli
steamed carrots
fresh baked whole wheat bread or corn bread*

Day four:

Noon Meal:
*Bowl of steamed rice with leftover beans
bread of your choice*

Evening Meal:
*Stuffed potatoes
egg custard*

Day five:

Noon Meal:
*Bowl of leftover soup
salad*

-RECIPES-

Evening Meal:
Soft chalupas
Spanish rice
fresh lettuce/tomato

Day six:

Noon Meal:
Leftover chalupas and
Spanish rice

Evening Meal:
Roasted red pepper linguini
garlic bread
green salad

Day seven:

Noon Meal:
Leftover roasted red pepper linguini

Evening Meal:
Grilled cheese sandwiches
oven fries

Day eight:

Noon Meal:
Roasted veggie sandwiches
potato salad

Evening Meal:
Butterbeans
Brussels sprouts in sauce
corn bread (reg. or Mexican)
Fresh corn on cob

Day nine:

Noon Meal:
Leftover butterbeans
steamed kale
fresh bread

Evening Meal:
Noodles Stroganoff
garlic bread
apple crepes

Day ten:

Noon Meal:
Cheese sandwiches or veggie burgers
potato casserole

Evening Meal:
Steamed veggies of choice
corn bread

Day eleven:

Noon Meal:
Taquitos

Evening Meal:
Mexican casserole
fresh tomato slices on a bed of lettuce

Day twelve:

Noon Meal:
Mexican sandwiches

Evening Meal:
Minestrone Soup
fresh bread
green salad

Day thirteen:

Noon Meal:
Leftover soup

Evening Meal:
Bean casserole w/whole wheat biscuits
green salad
bread pudding

Day fourteen:

Noon Meal:
Leftover casserole

Evening Meal:
Leftover soup

BREAKFAST

PANCAKES

1/2 cup whole wheat flour
1/2 cup unbleached flour
1 tablespoon baking powder
1/2 teaspoon salt
1/2 teaspoon baking soda

3 egg whites
1 cup buttermilk (slightly overflowing)

Combine and mix dry ingredients. Add egg whites and buttermilk. Mix well. Cook on griddle until golden brown, turning only once. Drizzle with pure maple syrup. Makes 6

Give thanks before and after eating.

BISCUITS
Inspired by Joy's mother

1 *cup whole wheat flour*
1 *cup unbleached flour*
1 *tablespoon baking powder*
1/2 *teaspoon salt*
1/4 *teaspoon soda*
1 *cup plus 1 tablespoon buttermilk*

Sift dry ingredients together into large bowl. Make well in bottom of bowl. Pour in buttermilk and slowly stir flour into center. Stir just until all dry ingredients are moistened. Remove from bowl onto floured board and knead approximately 12 to15 times. Sprinkle with flour if too sticky. Pat or roll out about 1 inch thick. Cut out with empty 10 oz. can (both ends removed - this makes a perfect size cutter).

Place into nonstick pan, or one that has been sprayed with vegetable spray. Bake in preheated hot oven 450 degrees for 13 to 15 minutes or until tops are brown. Makes 8.

FRENCH TOAST

1 ripe banana
1/2 cup orange juice
1 teaspoon vanilla
Pinch of ground cinnamon

4 slices whole wheat bread, preferably a few days old

Blend all ingredients, except bread, in a food processor or blender until smooth. Pour mixture into a shallow pan or bowl.

Preheat a non-stick griddle or skillet over medium heat. Coat with non-stick cooking spray.

Place bread in a pan and turn gently several times until bread is completely saturated. Place on griddle and drizzle with any remaining banana mixture. Cook until lightly brown on both sides. Serves 2.

PITA EGGS

1 small tomato, chopped
1 small onion, chopped
2 tablespoons green bell pepper, chopped
2 cups Egg Substitute
1/2 cup 1% cottage cheese
1/4 teaspoon salt
1/4 teaspoon pepper
2 pita breads (4 halves)

Coat a 10-inch skillet with non-stick cooking spray. Cook tomato, onion and bell pepper in 1 tablespoon of water over medium heat for 4-5 minutes until tender.

Combine eggs, cottage cheese, salt and pepper in a small bowl; stir well, and pour over vegetables.

Cook mixture over medium heat, until eggs are firm but moist. Soon into pita breads. Serves 2.

TAQUITOS

Fat free flour tortillas
2 cups cooked pinto beans (may use canned)
1/8 teaspoon cumin
1 tablespoon fresh cilantro (optional)
Salt to taste

Mash beans by hand or food processor. Add cumin, cilantro and salt. Set aside.

HASH BROWNS

2-3 medium size red potatoes
Salt and pepper to taste

Dice potatoes into small pieces (a Smart or Quick Chopper is great to use).

Coat a skillet with cooking spray. Cover and cook over medium heat until tender and well browned, stirring as needed. Add minced onions if desired.

Heat flour tortillas (can wrap in foil and heat in oven, or wrap in wet paper towel and heat one at a time for 20 seconds in microwave).

Spread heated beans on tortillas and potatoes on top of beans. Fold tortillas (add salsa if you like). Enjoy. Makes 4.

• A healthier version would be to substitute corn tortillas for flour tortillas. Flour tortillas are made with refined flour.

BREAD

MEXICAN CORN BREAD

1 cup fresh cooked or frozen corn

3 egg whites
1 cup buttermilk

1 1/3 cups whole wheat flour
1 tablespoon baking powder
1/4 teaspoon baking soda
2 tablespoons honey
1 teaspoon salt
2/3 cup stone ground yellow corn meal
2 fresh jalapeno chilies, cored, seeded, and minced
1/4 cup finely chopped cilantro

Preheat oven to 350 degrees. Brush a 9-inch cast-iron skillet or baking pan with a little olive oil and place it in the oven to preheat. Combine the egg whites and buttermilk in a large bowl and whisk until well mixed. Sift the flour, baking powder, honey, and 1 teaspoon of salt into the liquid ingredients. Add corn meal and gentle stir with a wooden spoon until the ingredients or just mixed (don't over mix). Stir in the corn, chili and cilantro. If the batter is too dry, add a small amount more of buttermilk. Spoon the batter into the hot skillet. Bake for 40 minutes, or until golden brown. Loosen the edges with a knife and turn out onto platter. Serves 6.

CORN BREAD
Inspired by Joy's mother

1 1/4 cups stone-ground yellow corn meal
1/2 cup whole wheat flour
2 1/2 teaspoons baking powder
1/4 teaspoon baking soda
1/2 teaspoon salt

2 large egg whites
1-1 1/4 cups buttermilk

Stir dry ingredients together. Add egg whites and buttermilk. Stir until mixed. Pour into hot cast iron skillet that has been sprayed with vegetable spray. Bake in hot preheated oven 450 degrees for 15 to 20 minutes. Serves 6.

Good health is often a matter of good judgment.

SALADS

FRESH FRUIT SALAD

2 apples, coarsely shredded
1 banana
2 naval oranges, peeled and cut into chunks
1/2 cup strawberries, if in season
1/2 cup pineapple chunks
2 tablespoons honey
1 tablespoon lemon juice

Sprinkle lemon juice over apples. Combine apples, banana, oranges, strawberries and pineapples.
Drizzle honey over fruit. Toss gently. Cover and chill.

To everything there is a season. Ecclesiastes: 3; 1.

CARROT AND APPLE SALAD

3 apples, shredded
2 carrots, shredded
1/4 cup non-fat mayonnaise
1 tablespoon fresh lemon juice
1 tablespoon honey

Shred apples and carrots in processor with shredding blade, or shred by hand on grater.   Add remaining ingredients. Stir to mix . Chill.

Whatsoever a man soweth, that shall he also reap.
Galatians: 6;7

POTATO SALAD

1 to 1 1/2 pounds red potatoes

1 small jar (2 oz.) pimientos
1 tablespoon Dijon mustard
2 tablespoons sweet pickle relish
1/4 cup blended cottage cheese
      Salt and freshly ground pepper to taste

Wash and scrub potatoes. Steam until tender. Cut in small chunks or lightly mash potatoes. Place potatoes in medium large bowl. Add remaining ingredients. Add chopped onions if desired. Chill. Serves 4.

BLENDED COTTAGE CHEESE: put in blender and process until smooth.

FLAX DRESSING

1/4 cup flax oil (Barlean's-plain)
1/4 cup water
3 tablespoons fresh lemon juice
2 tablespoons fresh basil
1 clove garlic, minced
   Freshly ground black pepper to taste

Combine all ingredients in a blender and mix thoroughly. We use our Braun hand chopper. This works great.

- May add raw/unfiltered apple cider vinegar, dijon mustard and different herbs.

Consider the nutritional value in this Flax Dressing! Flax oil (EFAs), lemon juice (vitamin C), garlic (artery cleanser).

SUGGESTED GREEN SALAD INGREDIENTS

Organic Romaine lettuce, Red cabbage
Carrot, Radishes
Tomatoes, Cucumber
Alfa sprouts, Spinach
Onion

- Romaine lettuce has twice as much beta carotene, and three and half times more vitamin C than Ice Berg lettuce; also, contains folate and iron.

REMEMBER - BUY ORGANIC

PASTA

RADIATORE PASTA
WITH ROASTED GARLIC

1 large head of garlic (about 4 ounces)
1-2 tablespoons water or broth
1 large red bell peppers, diced
2 large carrots, thinly sliced
3 tablespoons flour
1 can fat-free chicken broth
1/4 can water
2 tablespoons fresh lemon juice
1/2 teaspoon freshly ground black pepper
1/2 teaspoon rosemary, crumbled
1/4 teaspoon salt
1/2 pound radiatore pasta
4 cups small broccoli florets
1/2 cup frozen peas, thawed
1/4 cup non-fat sour cream
2 tablespoons fresh basil, chopped

Preheat the oven to 425 degrees. Wrap the garlic in aluminum foil and bake until the garlic is soft, about 30 minutes. When cool enough to handle, slice off the top of the garlic head and squeeze out the garlic pulp. Mince.
Meanwhile, in a large non-stick skillet, warm the water over medium heat until hot. Add the bell peppers and carrots, and cook, stirring frequently, until the vegetables are crisp-tender, about 4 minutes. Stir in the flour and

cook, stirring constantly, until the vegetables are coated with flour, about 1 minute.

Gradually stir in the diluted chicken broth, lemon juice, black pepper, rosemary and salt. Stir in the mashed garlic and cook until the sauce is lightly thickened, about 4 minutes.

Meanwhile, cook the pasta in a large pot of boiling water until al dente, 9 to 11 minutes, or according to package directions. Drain.

Add the broccoli to the skillet and cook until crisp-tender, about 2 minutes. Add the peas and cook until heated through, about 1 minute. Swirl in the sour cream and remove from the heat.

Add pasta and toss well. Serves 4.

- Red bell pepper has up to 11 times more beta carotene and one-and-a-half times more vitamin C then green ones, ounce for ounce.

FETTUCCINE WITH
SUN-DRIED TOMATOES
One of Ron's favorite

1/2 lb. fettuccine
1/2 cup coarsely chopped sun-dried-tomatoes
(dry packaged type)
1 cup non-fat chicken broth

1/2 cup sliced mushrooms (optional)
1/2 onion sliced into rings
4 cloves garlic, finely chopped
1/4 cup dry red wine

3/4 cup evaporated skim milk
1/4 water
4 teaspoons cornstarch
2 tablespoons chopped fresh basil leaves
or 1/2 teaspoon dried
Salt to taste

Mix tomatoes and broth; let stand 30 minutes. Cook mushrooms, onions and garlic in wine in 10-inch nonstick skillet over medium heat about 3 minutes, stirring occasionally, until mushrooms and onions are tender.

Add tomato mixture. Heat to boiling; reduce heat. Cover and simmer about 10 minutes, stirring occasionally. Meanwhile, cook fettuccine as directed on package; drain.

Mix milk, water, cornstarch and basil; stir into tomato mixture in skillet. Heat to boiling, stirring constantly. Boil and stir 1 minute. Mix with fettuccine and serve.
Serves 4.

ROASTED RED PEPPER LINGUINI

2 red bell peppers
12 ripe roma tomatoes, chopped
6 cloves garlic
1/2 cup chopped yellow onion
1 tablespoon balsamic vinegar
1/2 teaspoon salt
  Freshly ground black pepper to taste
1/4 - 1/2 teaspoon red hot chili flakes
2 tablespoons freshly chopped basil
2 tablespoons freshly chopped parsley
1/2-3/4 lb. linguini

Cut the peppers in half and remove stem and seeds. Roast under the broiler on foil lined pan, turning frequently until the skins are charred and blackened. Place in a paper bag and close tightly for 10 to 15 minutes (or bowl with lid). When the peppers are cool, remove from the bag and peel. The skin will come off easily. Place the peppers in a food processor with 1 cup of the tomatoes.

Wrap garlic in foil and roast the garlic cloves in the oven at 350 degrees for 30 minutes. Remove the skins and place the garlic in a food processor with the onions, pepper mixture, balsamic vinegar, salt and pepper. Process for 20 seconds.

Transfer the mixture to a medium-sized saucepan. Add the rest of the tomatoes, and red chili flakes, and simmer for 5 minutes. Add the fresh basil leaves and parsley, then remove from the heat. Serves 4.

VEGETABLE FUSILLI
WITH TOMATO PESTO

1 cup (firmly packed) basil leaves
1 teaspoon fresh thyme or 1/4 teaspoon dried thyme
2 garlic cloves, peeled
1/2 cup fat-free chicken broth, canned or homemade
2 tablespoons tomato paste
1/2 lb. short fusilli pasta (twists)
4 cups broccoli florets
2 carrots, sliced into thin strips
1 red bell pepper, cut into thin strips
2 cups diced tomatoes
1/2 teaspoon salt
1/2 teaspoon freshly ground black pepper
1/4 teaspoon dried red chili flakes
       Grated non-fat Parmesan cheese

In a food processor, combine the basil, thyme, garlic, chicken broth and tomato paste, and process until pureed. Transfer the tomato pesto to a large serving bowl. Place pasta in a large pot of boiling water. Cook 4 minutes, add the broccoli, carrots and bell peppers and cook 5 minutes longer. Drain in a colander. Stir the tomatoes, salt, pepper and chili flakes into the tomato pesto. Add the pasta and the vegetables. Toss to coat. Sprinkle with Parmesan cheese. Serves 4.

NOODLES STROGANOFF

1/2 lb. spinach fettuccine
2 tablespoons fat-free chicken broth or water
2 tablespoons onion, minced
2 cloves garlic, minced
1 1/2 cups mushrooms (optional)
1 bunch fresh spinach, stemmed, well washed, and
   coarsely chopped
1 1/4 cups non-fat sour cream
1/4 cup grated non-fat Parmesan cheese
2 tablespoons minced fresh basil, or 1 1/2 teaspoons
   dried basil leaves
2 teaspoons fresh oregano, or 1/2 teaspoon dried
   oregano
1 tablespoon freshly squeezed lemon juice
   Dash nutmeg
   Salt and freshly ground pepper to taste

Cook the spinach noodles al dente. In the meantime, place chicken broth in a large skillet and cook garlic, onions and mushrooms over medium heat until the mushrooms are about half done. Add the spinach, cover, and cook over low heat until it has wilted. Add the cooked noodles and the remaining ingredients and simmer over low heat for about 10 minutes. Serves 4.

• Spinach is a good source of beta carotene. Researchers say spinach protects the eyes and may prevent cataracts. Also, spinach is rich in vitamin C, iron, folate and potassium.

WHOLE WHEAT PASTA
WITH RED PEPPER SAUCE

3 *large red bell peppers*
1/2 *lb. whole wheat pasta (small shapes such
    as shells or twists)*
1 *tablespoon water, broth or dry white wine*
2 *cloves garlic, minced*
2 *medium very ripe tomatoes*
2 *tablespoons flour*
1 *cup soymilk or skim milk*
2-3 *tablespoons fresh basil, chopped*
2 *tablespoons fresh oregano, chopped*
1 *tablespoon red wine vinegar*
    Salt and freshly ground pepper to taste

Slice the peppers in half and remove stem and seeds. Place on foil-lined pan, skin side up, and broil under broiler until skin is charred well. Let cool in closed paper bag. Remove skin. Process in food processor for a few seconds and set aside.

Sauté garlic in water over medium heat for 1 minutes. Add tomatoes and cook until a little soft.

Sprinkle in flour and stir until dissolved. Reduce heat and slowly stir in the soymilk.

Meanwhile, cook pasta al dente. Drain.

Add peppers, basil and oregano and cook, stirring, until the sauce thickens, about 5 to 8 minutes.

Remove from heat and stir in the vinegar. Pour over pasta and toss well. Season to taste with salt and pepper.

Serves 4 to 6.

CHICKEN SPAGHETTI

CHICKEN BROTH

3 lbs. chicken parts, skin removed
5 cups water
1 onion, halved
1 carrot, cut into chunks
2 bay leaves
3-4 sprigs fresh parsley
1 clove garlic, halved
1 celery stalk, cut into chunks

Put chicken in soup pot with remaining ingredients. Bring to a boil. Reduce heat; cover and simmer for 2 hours. Cool and defat broth with fat separator or refrigerate for several hours and skim off fat that has risen to surface. Reserve 4 1/2 cups of broth.
Discard chicken or give to your dog.

This recipe is much less time consuming if you make the broth the previous day.

While this is cooking, make Cream of Mushroom Soup.

CREAM OF MUSHROOM SOUP

1 8-oz. can mushrooms
3 tablespoons flour
1 bay leaf
1/2 cup skim milk
1 tablespoon Butterbuds
1/8 teaspoon garlic powder

Drain liquid from mushrooms and set aside.   In small sauce pan over medium heat, add flour and 4 to 5 tablespoons of mushroom liquid until blended well. Gradually add remaining mushroom liquid, bay leaf, milk, and Butterbuds stirring constantly until mixture thickens, about 3 minutes. Remove and discard bay leaf.

Pour into a blender or food processor and blend until smooth.   Add 3/4 can of mushrooms and garlic powder. Blend until pureed.

Sauce Ingredients:

1 *cup onion, chopped*
2 *cups celery, chopped*
2 *6-oz. cans tomato paste*
1 *10-oz, can Rotel tomatoes*
1 *teaspoon paprika*
1 *teaspoon chili powder*

Coat a soup pot with vegetable spray.

Sauté onion and celery with 2 tablespoons of chicken broth over medium until tender.

Add cream of mushroom soup.

Stir in remaining ingredients except broth.

Put 1/2 cup of broth in a jar with lid, and add 6 tablespoons of flour and shake until smooth.   Add to remaining broth and stir well. Put into pot of mixture and simmer for 10 minutes. Meanwhile, cook one pound of *thin* spaghetti. Add to mixture and serve. Serves 8 to 10.

After you have reversed your heart disease, you can add 1 to 2 cups of chopped chicken breasts. This is the only recipe with meat that we use; about twice a year.

MANICOTTI WITH GREEN CHILIES

8 uncooked manicotti shells
1 cup 1% cottage cheese
1/4 cup non-fat grated Parmesan cheese
2 tablespoons fresh parsley, chopped
2 tablespoons fresh basil, chopped
1 clove garlic, minced
1/4 onion, minced
1/2 teaspoon oregano leaves
1/8 teaspoon cayenne pepper
1 14-1/2-oz. can tomatoes, chopped, undrained
1 6-oz. can tomato paste
1 4-oz. can diced green chilies
1 tablespoon corn starch
   Salt and freshly ground pepper to taste

Cook manicotti as directed on package. Drain. Place in a single layer on foil to prevent the tubes from sticking together and set aside.

Lightly spray a 12 by 8 inch baking dish with cooking spray. Heat oven to 350 degrees. In medium bowl, combine cottage cheese, Parmesan cheese, parsley, basil, oregano and cayenne; blend well. Spoon mixture into shells; place side by side in baking dish.

In medium sauce pan, combine tomatoes, tomato paste, green chilies and corn starch. Cook until mixture boils and thickens, stirring constantly. Add salt and pepper. Pour over filled manicotti in baking dish. Cover and bake at 350 degrees for 40 minutes. Serves 4.

LASAGNA ROLLS

8-oz. package curly lasagna noodles
1 medium-size onion, finely chopped
1 28-oz. can tomatoes
1 6-oz. can tomato paste
2 cloves garlic, minced
1/2 teaspoon Italian herb seasoning
    Salt and freshly ground pepper to taste
1 10-oz. package frozen chopped spinach
1 15-oz. container fat-free ricotta cheese
2 tablespoons grated Parmesan cheese

Coat a non-stick skillet with cooking spray over medium heat adding 1 tablespoon of water. Cook onion until tender. Add tomatoes, tomato paste, herbs and 3/4 cup of water; over high heat, heat to boiling, reduce heat low; cover and simmer for 15 minutes, stirring occasionally. Add salt and pepper.

Meanwhile, cook lasagna noodles as label directs.

Prepare spinach as label directs; drain in colander. Press spinach until very dry. Preheat oven to 375 degrees. Spoon sauce into 13 by 9 inch baking dish.

In bowl, mix spinach, ricotta cheese, Parmesan cheese, salt and pepper.

Spread rounded 1/4 cup ricotta filling on each lasagna noodle and roll jelly-roll fashion. With serrated knife, slice each rolled noodle crosswise in half.

Arrange rolls, cut-side down, in sauce in casserole in 1 layer. Cover dish loosely with foil; bake 35 to 40 minutes until hot and bubbly. Serves 6 to 8.

FETTUCCINE AND VEGETABLES
WITH PESTO

1 cup fresh Italian parsley (cannot substitute w/dried)
2 tablespoons pine nuts
2 tablespoons grated non-fat Parmesan cheese
1/2 cup fresh squeezed lemon juice
1 teaspoon flaxseed oil (optional)
1/2 teaspoon freshly ground black pepper
1/4 teaspoon salt
2 cloves garlic
2 cups carrot sticks
1 bell pepper, thinly sliced
1 zucchini, sliced
1/2 cup non-fat chicken broth
1/2 lb. fettuccine

In a food processor or blender, combine the parsley, pine nuts, Parmesan cheese, lemon juice, flaxseed oil, garlic, salt and pepper. Puree until blended well. Set aside.

In large skillet combine carrots, bell pepper, zucchini and chicken broth. Bring to a boil, reduce heat and simmer covered. Stirring occasionally until vegetables are tender, about 7 minutes. Remove from heat.

Meanwhile, cook the pasta according to package directions, about 9 minutes. Reserving 1/4 cup of the pasta cooking liquid, drain the pasta.

Stir the reserved pasta liquid into the pesto. Stir pesto into the vegetable mixture. Add pasta and toss to coat. Serves 4.

PASTA SAUCE
(For spaghetti or any pasta)

1/2 cup onion, chopped
3 cloves garlic, minced

1 14 1/2-oz. can diced tomatoes
2 6-oz. cans tomato paste
3/4 cup water
1 teaspoon salt
1 tablespoon fresh oregano, chopped, or 1 teaspoon
   dried
1 tablespoon fresh basil, chopped, or 1 teaspoon dried
1 tablespoon fresh parsley, chopped, or 1 teaspoon
   dried
1/4 cup dry red wine
1 teaspoon rosemary, chopped, or 1/2 teaspoon dried
   Salt and freshly ground pepper to taste

Coat a non-stick skillet with cooking spray.

Sauté onion and garlic in 1 tablespoon of water, over medium heat. Add remaining ingredients and simmer uncovered for 40 minutes. Add wine and cook covered fifteen minutes more. Serve over your favorite pasta.

• Remember, you can substitute dry herbs for fresh herbs.

PESTO I

1 *cup fresh basil leaves*
1 *clove garlic*
1/4 *cup pine nuts*
1/2 *cup flat-leaf fresh parsley*
1 *tablespoon fresh squeezed lemon juice*
2 *tablespoons non-fat Parmesan cheese*

Put all ingredients in blender. Process to mix. Season to salt and freshly ground pepper and process to the desired consistency. Let stand 5 minutes before serving.

- Must always use fresh herbs for pesto. Cannot substitute dried.

- Cook an 8-oz. package of organic Lemon and Pepper fettucini (we use Tree of Life brand, you can find at your health food store). While the pasta cooks, thin the pesto with a few tablespoons of the pasta cooking water. Drain pasta and coat with one tablespoon of flax oil. Add 2 tablespoons pesto, toss and serve. May add non-fat Parmesan cheese if desired.

PESTO II

2 cups fresh basil leaves
3 tablespoons fresh oregano
2 cloves garlic
1/4 cup non-fat Parmesan cheese
1/4 cup walnuts

Combine all ingredients in blender. Process to mix. Season to taste with salt and freshly ground pepper and process to the desired consistency. Let stand for 5 minutes before serving.

- Freeze in a one fourth cup quantity to use year-round. A little goes a long way. Bring frozen pesto to room temperature before using. Thin with a few tablespoons of the pasta cooking water. May use pesto with any pasta or soup.

- Must always use fresh herbs for pesto. Cannot substitute dried.

You really need to grow your own herbs, especially basil, to make pesto.

SOUPS

ORGANIC TOMATO
AND BASIL SOUP

5 organic tomatoes, peeled and seeded
1 medium onion, diced
6 garlic cloves, peeled

1/2 teaspoon salt
1 teaspoon fresh rosemary, or 1/4 teaspoon dried
1 cup water
1/2 cup tomato puree

1/2 cup tightly packed fresh basil leaves
   Freshly ground black pepper to taste

Coat a large skillet with cooking spray; place over medium heat until hot.

Sauté onion and garlic until tender. Add all remaining ingredients, except basil, and cook 15 more minutes. Add basil and cook 2 minutes only.

Puree in blender or food processor; 2 cups at a time. Remember to vent blender whenever blending anything hot. This allows steam to escape so it will not blow the top off.

Bring to a boil, reduce heat, and simmer 20-30 minutes, stirring occasionally. Serves 4.

CHUNKY STEW

1 16 oz. can kidney beans
4 tomatoes
2 onions, minced
4 cloves garlic, minced
1/2 teaspoon ground cumin
1 teaspoon minced fresh parsley
1/2 teaspoon dried oregano
1 tablespoon vegetable broth or water
6 cups hot water or vegetable broth
2 ribs celery with greens
1 each-red, green and yellow bell peppers
1 red onion
1 teaspoon fresh chopped cilantro

Rinse and drain beans. Set aside. Plunge tomatoes into boiling water for 30 seconds. Remove with a slotted spoon and transfer to a bowl of ice water. Remove from water, slip off and discard skins. Chop tomatoes and set aside.

Sauté onions and garlic with cumin, parsley and oregano in one tablespoon vegetable broth or water in a stock pot until tender, about 2 minutes.

Add hot water, celery and beans. Bring to a boil.

Add tomatoes, reduce heat and simmer for 2 hours (the longer it simmers the thicker it gets). Remove from heat.

Cut bell peppers and red onion into chunks and set aside.

Before serving, add bell peppers, red onion and cilantro to stew and let simmer until heated through, about 20 minutes. Serves 4-6

VEGETABLE LENTIL SOUP

2 tablespoons water or broth
1 onion, chopped
4 cloves garlic, minced fine
3 medium potatoes, scrubbed, unpeeled and cubed
4 cups shredded cabbage
1 cup celery, chopped
1 cup carrots, sliced
7 cups water
1 teaspoon cumin
1 15-oz. can tomato sauce
1 cup lentil, uncooked
1/2 cup chopped fresh cilantro
2 small jalapeno peppers
1 bay leaf
1/3 cup sun-dried tomatoes, chopped
   Salt and freshly ground pepper to taste

Soak tomatoes for 30 minutes in warm water.

In a large soup pot over medium heat, sauté onions, celery, carrots and garlic in water. Cook and stir frequently until carrots are crisp tender. Add small amount of water if necessary to prevent sticking.

Add remaining ingredients, except cilantro, salt and pepper. Bring to a boil. Reduce heat to medium-low, cover, and simmer one hour or until vegetables are tender. Add cilantro to last 10 minutes. Add salt and pepper to taste.

Discard bay left before serving.

Serves 8-10.

•   This is good served with crisp tortillas.

POTATO AND BEAN STEW

2 tablespoons tomato paste
2 tablespoons lemon juice
1/2 teaspoon each ground cumin and ground cinnamon
1/2 teaspoon ground coriander
1/4 teaspoon each ground cardamom and ground cloves
1/8 teaspoon cayenne pepper, or more to taste
3 cups water

1 tablespoon water
3 cloves garlic, crushed
1 teaspoon grated fresh ginger root
2 1-pound cans kidney beans, rinsed and drained
1 1/2 pounds potatoes, unpeeled, cut into 1-inch cubes
    (3 medium potatoes)
2 bay leaves
    Salt to taste

In a small bowl, combine tomato paste, lemon juice, spices, and water. Mix well.

Heat water in a large saucepan over medium heat. Cook garlic and ginger root for 1 minute. Stir in remaining ingredients. Mix well.

Bring to a boil, cover, reduce heat and simmer 1 hour or until potatoes are tender. Discard bay leaves. Add salt to taste. Serves 6.

MINESTRONE SOUP

1/4 cup pink beans, dried
1/4 cup pinto beans, dried
1/4 cup Great Northern white beans, dried
1/4 cup red beans, dried
1/4 cup lima beans, dried
6 cups water
2 bay leaves
1/4 onion, finely chopped
3 cloves garlic, minced
1 cup chopped celery with leaves
6 medium tomatoes, chopped
1/4 cup fresh parsley, chopped
1 tablespoon fresh basil
1 teaspoon fresh oregano
2 zucchini, sliced
3 cups shredded cabbage
1 fresh jalapena, minced
1/2 cup uncooked whole wheat macaroni or shells
    Salt and freshly ground pepper to taste
2 tablespoons red wine vinegar

Wash and sort beans. Cover with several inches of water and soak overnight in a soup pot. Drain beans and return to pot.

Add water and bring to a boil. Reduce heat and simmer for 2 hours. Add all remaining ingredients except for salt, pepper and vinegar. Continue cooking for about 30 minutes. Add macaroni 10 minutes before serving. Simmer until macaroni is tender. Add salt, pepper and vinegar. Serves 8 to 10.

SPLIT PEA SOUP

1 *lb. dried split green peas, rinsed and drained*
8 *cups water*
2 *carrots, sliced into 1-inch pieces*
1 *medium onion quartered*
3 *cloves garlic, chopped*
2 *stalks celery with leaves, cut into chunks*
1 *tablespoon fresh basil, chopped*
1 *tablespoon fresh parsley, chopped*
1 *teaspoon fresh oregano, chopped*
1 *teaspoon thyme, chopped*
1 *teaspoon rosemary, chopped*
1/2 *teaspoon fresh ginger, grated*
2 *bay leaves*
  Salt and freshly grounded black pepper to taste

In a soup pot, bring peas, water, carrots, onions, garlic, celery and bay leaves to a boil over medium-high heat. Reduce heat and cook, covered, at a gently rolling boil 1-1 1/2 hours until tender. Remove bay leaves.

Add remaining ingredients. Simmer 10 minutes to blend flavors. In a blender or a food processor, fitted with a metal blade, process 2-3 cups at a time, until pureed. Or, if you have a hand blender, you can just stick it in the pot of soup and blend. Serves 10.

• Celery helps to renew bones and arteries.

CREAM OF BROCCOLI SOUP

1 large bundle broccoli
1/2 cup fat-free chicken broth
2 12 oz. cans evaporated skim milk
2 tablespoons onion, minced fine
2 tablespoons flour
3 tablespoons fresh basil, chopped
   Freshly ground black pepper

Bring the broth to a boil in a medium saucepan over medium heat. Add the broccoli and cook for 5-6 minutes, until fork tender.

Pour the evaporated milk in a small saucepan. Warm over low heat, just until bubbles begin to form around the edge. Remove from heat.

Coat a large, heavy sauce pan over medium heat. Sauté onions in 1 to 2 tablespoons chicken broth until tender. Stir in the flour and cook for 1 minute. Whisk in the warm evaporated milk. Continue to cook, whisking constantly, until the flour has dissolved and the mixture is smooth.

Reduce the heat to low. Add the garlic, and the broccoli, along with its cooking liquid. Simmer for 5 minutes more, being careful not to bring the soup to a boil. Remove pan from the heat and stir in the basil and black pepper. Serves 4.

- One stalk of broccoli has more calcium than a 1/2 cup serving of cottage cheese, and more vitamin C than a navel orange. Is a good source of iron, and also contains potassium, riboflavin and folic acid. It also has more insoluble fiber than cauliflower, spinach, green beans or cabbage.

CORN CHOWDER
So Easy.

2 10-oz. packages frozen corn kernels, thawed
1 cup water
1 clove garlic, minced
2 tablespoons minced onion
1 12-oz. can evaporated skimmed milk
1/2 cup water
    Pinch of red pepper
1 teaspoon fresh basil, chopped
1/2 teaspoon fresh rosemary, chopped
1 tablespoon honey
1 tablespoon corn starch
    Salt and freshly ground pepper to taste

Puree corn kernels with 1 cup of water. Bring pureed corn and all the remaining ingredients to a boil in a non-stick pot. Reduce heat and simmer over low heat for 10 to 15 minutes. Serves 2 to 3.

He who has health has hope; and he who has hope has everything.

PESTO VEGETABLE SOUP

1 can vegetable broth
4 1/2 cups water
1 onion, chopped
3 cups potatoes, diced
2 cups cut green beans
3 tomatoes, chopped
2 carrots, sliced
1/2 teaspoon salt
1 teaspoon black pepper
1/2 cup uncooked vermicelli

Pesto

3 cloves garlic, chopped
1/4 cup fresh sweet basil leaves
1 tomato, chopped
1/4 cup reserved vegetable broth

Combine all soup ingredients, except vermicelli, in a stock pot. Bring to a boil. Cover, reduce heat and simmer until vegetables nearly tender, about 20 minutes. Remove 1/4 cup of broth and set aside. Stir in vermicelli and simmer until al dente, about 10 minutes.

To make Pesto:
Puree all pesto ingredients in a food processor or blender. Stir into hot soup. Serves 6.

BROWN RICE
AND LENTIL SOUP

2/3 cup raw lentils, sorted and rinsed
1/2 cup raw brown rice
2 cloves garlic, minced
2 tablespoons lite soy sauce
2 bay leaves
6 1/2 cups water
1 small onion, finely chopped
2 medium carrots, thinly sliced
1 large celery stalk, finely chopped w/leaves
14-1/2 oz. can tomatoes, chopped
1/4 cup dry red wine
1 tablespoon fresh basil or 1 teaspoon dried
1 teaspoon paprika
2 teaspoons fresh oregano or 1/2 teaspoon dried
2 teaspoon fresh thyme or 1/2 teaspoon dried

Salt and freshly ground pepper to taste

Place all of the ingredients, except salt and pepper, in a soup pot. Bring to a boil, reduce heat and simmer for 45 minutes. Remove bay leaves. Add salt and pepper to taste. Serves 6 to 8.

- The plastic bag your newspaper comes in makes a perfect size for storing celery.

WHITE BEAN SOUP

2 cups dry Great Northern beans
   Water
5 cups water
1 can fat-free chicken broth
1 tablespoon fresh thyme, chopped, or 1 teaspoon
   thyme leaves
1/2 teaspoon salt, if desired
1 medium onion, chopped
2 garlic cloves, minced
1 bay leaf
1 medium carrot, sliced
1 stalk celery
1/4 cup fresh parsley, chopped
1/4 cup fresh basil, chopped
1 medium tomato, chopped

Wash, sort and soak beans overnight.

Drain and add 5 cups fresh water, chicken broth, thyme, salt, onion, garlic and bay leaf. Bring to a boil. Reduce heat; cover and simmer 1 hour. Remove bay leaf. Remove 2 cups bean mixture and place in food processor bowl with metal blade or blender container; puree until smooth. To bean mixture in Dutch oven, or soup pot, add carrot, celery and pureed mixture. Cover; simmer an additional 30 minutes or until vegetables are tender.

Just before serving, stir in parsley, basil and tomato. Serves 6.

SUMMER HARVEST SOUP
Make this soup in the summer
when you can get vine-ripened tomatoes

1/2 cup onion, chopped
4 garlic cloves, minced
3 large red bell peppers, cut into thin strips
1 1/2 pounds tomatoes, cut into chunks
1 medium zucchini, sliced
1 small yellow summer squash, sliced
1/2 cup fat-free chicken broth, canned or homemade
1 19-oz. can cannellini or white kidney beans, rinsed and
    drained
1/2 cup fresh basil, coarsely chopped

Coat a soup pot with cooking spray.

Over medium-high heat, sauté the onions and garlic, 1 to 2 minutes. Stir in the bell pepper strips and sauté until they are crisp-tender. Adding small amounts of broth or water as needed.

Add the tomatoes and increase the heat to high. Cover and cook, stirring often, until the tomatoes begin to release their juices, about 5 minutes.

Stir in the zucchini, summer squash and chicken broth, and bring to a boil. Reduce the heat to medium, cover and cook until the vegetables are tender, about 10 minutes.

Stir in the beans and basil, cover and cook until heated through, 2 to 3 minutes. Serves 4.

HARDY BEAN
AND VEGETABLE SOUP

1 cup pinto, dried
1 cup Great Northern beans, dried

8 cups water
1 tablespoon water
1 cup onion, diced
2 cups carrots, diced
1 cup celery, diced
5 cloves garlic, minced
3 14-1/2-oz. cans fat-free chicken broth
2 cups water
4 cups cabbage, coarsely chopped
1/2 teaspoon salt
1/4 teaspoon freshly ground pepper
3 cups potatoes, cubed
5 cups spinach, coarsely chopped

Wash and sort beans. Soak in water to cover by 2 inches in soup pot overnight. Drain and rinse. Add 8 cups fresh water and bring to boil; reduce heat, cover and simmer until beans are almost tender, 45 minutes. Drain.

Heat water in large soup pot or Dutch oven. Add vegetables. Cook, stirring occasionally, over medium heat until tender, about 10 minutes.

Add chicken broth, cabbage, the cooked beans, salt, pepper, and potatoes. Bring to boil; reduce heat and simmer covered 30 minutes. Stir in spinach; cook 2 minutes more. Makes 16 cups.

VEGETABLE CHILI

Vegetable cooking spray
1 *lb. dried black beans, or pinto, uncooked*
1 *cup onion, chopped*
1 *cup green bell pepper, chopped*
5 *cloves garlic, minced*
1 *28-oz. can tomatoes, chopped*
2 *tablespoons fresh oregano, or 1 tablespoon dried*
2 *tablespoons chili powder*
1 *tablespoon ground cumin*
2 *teaspoons paprika*
1 *teaspoon ground coriander*
1 *bay leaf*
1/2 *teaspoon salt*
4 *cups water*
1 *6-oz. can tomato paste*

1 *tablespoon red wine vinegar*

Wash, sort and soak beans overnight, adding enough water to cover beans by around 3 inches. Drain beans. Spray pan with vegetable spray. In a soup pot, sauté onion, garlic and green pepper.

Add all remaining ingredients except red wine vinegar. Bring to a boil, reduce heat and simmer until tender about 2 hours. Add vinegar approximately 30 minutes before they are finished cooking. Discard bay leaf. Serves 6 to 8.

MEXICAN STEW
Very Spicy - Very Good

1/2 cup onion, chopped
1/2 cup celery, chopped
2 cloves garlic, minced
1 14-1/2-oz. can beef broth, visible fat removed
3 cups water
1 15-oz. can kidney beans, undrained
1 can Rotel tomatoes
2 bay leaves
1/2 teaspoon salt
1 tablespoon fresh oregano or 1 teaspoon dried
1 tablespoon ground coriander
1 teaspoon cumin
5 carrots, cut in chunks
3 medium potatoes, cut into cubes
1 10-oz. package frozen whole kernel corn, thawed
1/2 head (small) cabbage, coarsely chopped
   Fresh cilantro

Coat a large pot with cooking spray.

Sauté onions, celery and garlic in 1 tablespoon water, or broth, over medium heat until tender. Add seasonings, broth and water. Add beans, Rotel tomatoes, carrots, potatoes, and cook until almost done. Add corn and layer cabbage wedges on top and cook until cabbage is done. Add 1/4 cup chopped cilantro. Remove bay leaves. Serves 6.

• For less heat, use 3/4 can rotel tomatoes.

VEGETABLES

BRUSSELS SPROUTS
WITH SAUCE

2-6 cups Brussels sprouts

1 tablespoon water
1 clove garlic, minced

1 teaspoon honey
1/3 cup red wine vinegar
3 tablespoons orange juice
1 1/2 teaspoons fresh thyme or 1/2 teaspoon dried
    Salt and freshly ground pepper to taste

Steam Brussels sprouts till crisp-tender. Set aside.
Heat water over medium heat and cook garlic for about 2
minutes. Add remaining ingredients; and cook about 2
minutes. Stir in Brussels sprouts turning to coat with
sauce. Serves 4.

• Brussels sprouts supply beta carotene, iron,
potassium, folate and fiber in addition to vitamin C.

STUFFED POTATOES

3-4 potatoes, baked
1/2 cup buttermilk
1 4-oz. can chopped green chilies
1/4 teaspoon garlic powder
   Salt and pepper to taste
1 bunch fresh broccoli, steamed
   Paprika
   Grated Parmesan cheese

Cut potatoes in half lengthwise and scoop out the insides, reserving the skins. Place the potato insides, green chilies, garlic powder, salt and pepper in a large bowl. Mash with a potato masher or whip with a hand mixer or blender. Add milk until consistency of thick mashed potatoes, using more or less of the milk. Stir in the broccoli and cheese. Divide this mixture among the potato skins. Sprinkle each with paprika and Parmesan.

Put the stuffed potatoes on a baking sheet. Bake at 400 degrees, until lightly brown, about 10 minutes. Serves 6-8.

PINTO BEANS

1 1/2 lbs. pinto beans
1/2 small onion, minced fine
2 cloves garlic, minced fine
2 small jalapeno peppers, minced fine
2 teaspoons fresh thyme or 1/2 teaspoon dried
2 teaspoons fresh oregano or 1/2 teaspoon dried
1 teaspoon apple vinegar (raw/unfiltered preferred)

Wash, sort and soak beans overnight. Drain and add fresh water to cover about 1 inch above beans. Bring to a boil and boil uncovered for 5-10 minutes. Skim off and discard foam. Reduce heat to simmer. Add onions, pepper and garlic (if using dried herbs, add now). Cook until almost done. Add fresh thyme, fresh oregano and vinegar. Continue cooking until tender but not mushy. Add salt to taste. Serves 10.

•   May omit thyme and oregano and use fresh cilantro.

Additional meal: Steam some brown rice and have a bowl of rice and beans served with corn bread or fresh home made whole wheat bread.

•   One quarter of a jalapeno pepper provides a good amount of vitamin C.

BUTTERBEANS

1 1/2 lbs. large butterbeans
1 teaspoon liquid smoke
1 small onion (whole)

Wash, sort and soak beans overnight. Drain and rinse. Put in large pot. Add enough water to cover about 1-inch above beans (you can always add additional if needed).

Bring to boil and boil for a few minutes, skim off foam and discord.

Add onion and liquid smoke.

Reduce heat to low and cook until tender, about 2 hours. Add salt and freshly ground pepper to taste. Serves 8 to 10.

Rest, relax, pray and enjoy!

BLACK BEANS

1 1/2 cups dried black beans
1 large onion, chopped
4 cloves garlic, minced
2 bay leaves
1/2 teaspoon oregano, dried
1/2 teaspoon thyme, dried
1/2 teaspoon cumin
1 teaspoon liquid smoke
1/3 cup sun-dried tomatoes, chopped
1/8 teaspoon cayenne pepper
1 cup water
2 ribs celery, chopped
     Salt and freshly ground pepper to taste
1 tablespoon red wine vinegar

Rinse and soak overnight in water to cover. Soak sun-dried tomatoes in warm water for 30 minutes. Sauté onion and garlic in a medium size sauce pan with 1 to 2 tablespoons of water. Add the drained beans, bay leaves, oregano, thyme, cayenne pepper, cumin, liquid smoke, sun-dried tomatoes and cup of water. Cover, bring to a boil, and simmer on low heat for 1 to 1 1/2 hours, or until the beans are tender.

The sauce should be thick, but not dry.

About 10 minutes before they are done, add the vinegar and cook until tender. Remove bay leaves and serve over hot brown rice.

Serves 4.

BAKED MEDLEY OF VEGETABLES

3 carrots, sliced thin
2 potatoes, diced
   Fresh green beans
   Fresh eggplant, cubed
1/2 small cauliflower
2 zucchini, sliced
1/2 small cabbage
1/2 green pepper, chopped
1 large onion, chopped
1 tablespoon fresh cilantro, chopped
1 teaspoon fresh thyme, chopped
1 cup chicken broth
   Salt and freshly ground pepper to taste

In a very large skillet over medium heat, sauté the onions in a small amount of chicken broth until tender. Layer vegetables in pan. Add herbs and pour chicken broth over top of vegetables. Cook 30 minutes uncovered. Serves 12.

- Cabbage is rich source of vitamin C; the outer leaves are concentrated in vitamin E and calcium.

OVEN FRIES

4-6 medium size red potatoes, unpeeled
Cajun seasoning to taste

Cut potatoes into small French-fry size. Place in large bowl. Sprinkle seasoning heavily over potatoes and toss to mix. Place on large non-stick baking pan. Place under hot broiler in oven. Cook until brown, approximately 10 to 15 minutes. Remove, turn potatoes over, and brown other side. If you are on a low-salt diet, just season with pepper.

Never eat yourself full. Overeating is not only wasteful, but is a primary cause of diabetes, and accelerates aging.

VEGETABLE STIR-FRY

3 tablespoons light soy sauce
2 tablespoons dry sherry
4 teaspoons cornstarch
1 teaspoon grated ginger root
1/8 teaspoon red pepper
2 cloves garlic, minced
1 1/2 cups broccoli, cut into floweretes
2 medium carrots, thinly sliced
1 medium onion, sliced
12 snow peas
1 cup fresh bean sprouts
2 cups hot cooked brown rice

Stir together soy sauce, sherry, cornstarch, ginger root, crushed red pepper and 2/3 cup water in a small mixing bowl. Set aside.

Spray a cold wok or large skillet with non-stick spray coating. Heat over medium heat. Add garlic; stir-fry for 15 seconds.   Add broccoli and carrots; stir-fry for 3 minutes. Add onion and snow peas; stir-fry for 3 minute. Add bean sprouts; stir-fry for 1 minute. Push vegetables from center of wok or skillet.

Stir soy sauce mixture; add to center of wok. Cook and stir till thickened and bubbly. Cook and stir 2 minutes more. Stir vegetables into sauce. Serve with hot cooked brown rice. Serves 4.

CASSEROLES

BEAN CASSEROLE
WITH WHOLE WHEAT BISCUITS

1 cup celery, chopped
1/2 cup onion, chopped
1 small green pepper, chopped
2 cloves garlic, minced
1 6-oz. can tomato paste
1/2 cup chicken broth or water
2 teaspoons fresh oregano or 1 teaspoon dried
2 teaspoons fresh parsley or 1 teaspoon dried
1/4 teaspoon salt
1 teaspoon paprika
1 teaspoon taco seasoning mix (optional)
   Pinch of red pepper
1 lb. can Great Northern beans, undrained
1 lb. can lima beans, undrained
1 tablespoon honey

Coat a large cast iron skillet with vegetable spray. Over medium heat with 1 tablespoon of broth or water, sauté onion, garlic, green pepper and celery until vegetables are tender. Add remaining ingredients.
Simmer while preparing biscuits.

For whole wheat biscuits, see following page.

WHOLE WHEAT BISCUITS
FOR CASSEROLE
See preceding page

1 cup whole wheat flour
1/2 cup unbleached flour
1 1/2 teaspoons baking powder
1/4 teaspoon salt
1/4 teaspoon baking soda
3/4 cup buttermilk

Makes 8 biscuits

Stir together into mixing bowl, flour, baking powder and salt. Add buttermilk and stir until dough clings together. Knead on floured surface 10 times, adding additional flour if necessary. Roll or pat out to about half inch thick. Cut out with cookie cutter. Place bean mixture into 13 by 9 inch baking dish, or a 11 inch round casserole. Top with biscuits. Bake at 425 degrees for 25 to 30 minutes until golden brown. Serves 6.

POTATO CASSEROLE

1 1/2 tablespoons dry red wine, water or chicken broth
2 onions, thinly sliced
4 large potatoes
   Salt and freshly ground black pepper
2-3 cups fat-free chicken broth
1/4 cup bread crumbs

Preheat the broiler.

Coat a cast iron skillet with cooking spray. Heat over medium heat; add onions and cook, stirring often. After they brown a little and begin to stick, add a little water and continue to sauté until softened.

Meanwhile, peel the potatoes and cut into 1/4" slices. Stir the potatoes into the onions and season with salt and pepper. Add enough stock to cover the potatoes and bring to a boil. Reduce the heat and simmer for 15 minutes, or until soft. Flatten the potatoes with a fork and sprinkle with bread crumbs. Place the pan under the broiler. Broil for 1 minute, or until the top is crusty and golden brown. Serves 4.

•   Potatoes are an excellent source of potassium.

CORN CASSEROLE

3 ears fresh corn (cut from cob)
1/4 cup green onions, chopped
1 cup egg substitute
1/2 cup evaporated skim milk
2 teaspoons fresh basil, chopped
   Salt and freshly ground pepper to taste
2 small tomatoes cut into wedges
4 slices non-fat cheddar cheese, cut into strips

Coat a non-stick skillet with cooking spray; place over medium high heat until hot. Add corn and green onions; sauté until tender. Combine egg substitute with milk, basil, salt and pepper; stir well.

Pour mixture over vegetables in skillet. Cover and cook for 15 minutes over medium low heat until mixture is almost set.

Arrange cheese strips and tomato wedges over top. Cover and cook until cheese melts; about 5 minutes. Serves 6.

TAMALE PIE

1/2 medium onion, chopped
1 medium green pepper, chopped
1 clove garlic, minced

1 tablespoon chili powder
2 16 oz. cans kidney beans, drained
1 16 oz. can corn, drained
1/2 teaspoon cumin
1/4 teaspoon salt
Dash of red pepper (cayenne)
1/4 cup fresh chopped cilantro

Sauté onions, green pepper, and garlic in a non-stick skillet with 1 to 2 tablespoons of water until crisp-tender. Add chili powder, beans, tomato and corn. Simmer for 10 minutes. Add cilantro. Put in a non-stick 9" by 13" baking pan or regular pan sprayed with cooking spray.

CORN BREAD TOPPING

1 cup yellow corn meal
1/3 cup whole wheat flour
1/4 teaspoon salt
2 teaspoons baking powder

2 egg whites
1/4 cup skim-milk

In medium bowl, stir dry ingredients together. Add egg whites and milk. Stir and spoon over mixture. Baked uncovered at 350 degrees for 20 minutes. Serves 8.

MEXICAN CASSEROLE

1 *quart enchilada sauce(recipe follows)*
20 *corn tortillas*

2 *cups refried beans*
1 *teaspoon fresh oregano or 1/4 dried*
1/4 *teaspoon cumin*

2 *cups 1% cottage cheese*
1 *teaspoon onion powder*
2 *cloves garlic, minced*
1/4 *teaspoon salt*

1 *10-oz. packed frozen corn kernels*
1/4 *cup fresh cilantro*
4 1/2- *ounce can-green chilie peppers*
4-6 *slices non-fat cheddar cheese*

Layer a 9-13 inch non-stick baking pan as follows: Pour 2/3 cup sauce into bottom of pan. Arrange 6 tortillas on top of sauce, pour beans on top of tortillas, cover beans with 6 more tortillas, and pour 1 cup sauce over tortillas. Mix together onion and garlic with cottage cheese and spoon over cheese mixture evenly on top of tortillas. Sprinkle corn and chilie peppers on top of cottage cheese, arrange remaining tortillas on top and pour 1 cup of sauce on top of tortillas. Bake in a 350 degree oven uncovered for 35 minutes, or until hot and bubbly. Serves 6-8.

ENCHILADA SAUCE

1 10-3/4 oz. can tomato puree
3 empty tomato puree cans water
1 clove garlic, minced
   Pinch cayenne pepper
1/4 cup onion, minced fine
2 teaspoons chili powder

1 tablespoon corn starch
2 tablespoons cold water

Cook first 6 ingredients in a medium size pan over medium heat until sauce comes to a boil. Reduce heat and simmer for 10 minutes. In a small bowl dissolve corn starch in water and gradually add, stirring constantly until sauce thickens a little.

SANDWICHES

MEXICAN SANDWICH

1 tablespoon water
1/2 cup chopped onions
2 cloves garlic, minced
2 cups cooked pinto beans
2 large tomatoes, chopped
1 tablespoon slivered almonds
1/2 teaspoon ground cumin
2 tablespoons cilantro, chopped
   Salt and pepper taste
   Pita bread
   Salsa

Oil a large non-stick skillet. Heat water over medium heat. Add onion and garlic. Cook, stirring frequently, until onion is tender.

Add beans, tomatoes, almonds, cumin, salt and pepper. Cook, stirring frequently, until mixture is hot. Serve in pita bread. Can be served chilled. Serves 6.

FRIED GREEN TOMATO
SANDWICHES
Great! - worth growing
your own tomatoes

3/4 cup buttermilk
1 large egg white

3/4 cup stone ground yellow corn meal
1/4 teaspoon salt
1/4 teaspoon cayenne pepper

2 large green tomatoes cut into 1/4-inch-thick slices
Vegetable spray

Romaine lettuce leaves
Whole wheat bread

Preheat oven to 450 degrees. In medium-sized bowl, whisk together buttermilk and egg white. In a shallow dish, mix together corn meal, salt, and cayenne pepper. Dip half of the tomato slices into the buttermilk mixture, then in the corn meal mixture. Turn each slice in the mixture to coat. In a large skillet sprayed with Pam over medium heat add tomato slices and cook until the undersides are golden brown, 4 to 5 minutes. Transfer the slices to a baking sheet browned-side up. Repeat the process with the remaining tomato slices. Bake the tomatoes in the hot oven for 10 to 12 minutes, or until well browned.

Use sandwich spread on next page. The spread makes this sandwich taste extra special. Serves 4.

SANDWICH SPREAD
For Fried Green Tomatoes - delicious!

2 tablespoons non-fat sour cream
1 tablespoon Dijon mustard
2 teaspoons fresh lemon juice
1/4 teaspoon cayenne pepper
1 tablespoon sweet pickle relish

Mix together and spread on bread.

Be grateful for the opportunity to cook for the nourishment and well-being of yourself and others. Cook simple meals. Allow plenty of time and don't overload yourself with complicated recipes.

GRILLED CHEESE SANDWICHES

Non-fat cheddar cheese slices
Whole wheat bread, or sour-dough bread from the deli
Vegetable spray

Lightly spray bread on one side. Place sprayed side down onto hot skillet or grill. Top with cheese and bread. Brown on both sides. Serve with oven fries.

Everything in creation is covered by heaven and supported by earth.

ROASTED VEGGIE SANDWICHES

1 *small red onion, sliced*
1 *medium zucchini*
1/2 *very small eggplant, thinly sliced*
1/2 *red sweet pepper, sliced into rings*
1/2 *cup fat-free Italian dressing*
1/4 *teaspoon freshly ground pepper*
2 *12-inch baguettes*

Place vegetables in large bowl. Sprinkle with pepper. Pour Italian dressing over vegetables and let marinade for thirty minutes. Meanwhile, prepare dressing. Drain vegetables. Place the vegetables on a baking sheet that has been lightly sprayed with cooking spray. Broil for 5 minutes, turn over and broil other side. Remove from oven; sprinkle with non-fat Parmesan cheese. Split baguette and spread with dressing. Fill with roasted vegetables.

DRESSING:

Place 2 tablespoons snipped sun-dried tomatoes in a small bowl; cover with boiling water and let stand 5 minutes. Drain. Combine 1/2 cup fat-free sour cream; drained tomatoes; 1 tablespoon snipped fresh basil; 1 teaspoon tomato paste; 1 large clove garlic, minced; 1/4 teaspoon dried thyme and 1 tablespoon lemon juice in a blender container. Cover and blend until smooth.

SOFT CHALUPAS

2 cups refried beans
6 corn tortillas
1 4.5 oz. can chopped green chilies
6 slices non-fat cheddar cheese
1/4 cup fresh cilantro, chopped

On a large baking sheet place the corn tortillas. Spread beans evenly over tortillas. Divide green chili over beans. Add chopped cilantro and top with cheese slices.
Bake at 450 degrees for 3-5 minutes. Serve with lettuce and diced tomatoes. We always serve these with Spanish Rice (preceding page). Serves 6.

Refried Beans

2 cups home cooked pinto beans, or canned
1/4 teaspoon cumin

Add cumin and mash by hand or use food processor.

- Corn tortillas are good for you. They contain calcium and fiber, plus the lime content helps absorption of the B vitamin niacin, which is good for the nerves and all-around cell growth.

RICE

BROWN RICE WITH VEGETABLES

1 1/2 cups brown rice
1 1/2 cups canned fat-free chicken broth
1 1/2 cups water
2 cups small broccoli florets
2 cups zucchini, sliced
1 cup red bell pepper strips
1 large tomato, diced
2 medium nectarines, cut into thin wedges
1/4 cup fresh basil, chopped
1/4 teaspoon salt
1/4 teaspoon freshly ground black pepper
1/2 teaspoon turmeric

Combine chicken broth and water. Add rice, and bring to a boil, reduce heat and simmer until all of the liquid is absorbed, about 45 minutes.

While the rice is cooking, coat a non-stick pan with vegetable spray. Heat oven medium-high heat. Add the broccoli, zucchini and bell pepper, and stir-fry about 4 minutes. Adding small amounts of water or broth if desired.

Add the tomato, nectarines, 2 tablespoons of the basil, the salt and pepper. Cover and cook until the vegetables are crisp-tender, about 2 minutes.

When the rice is done, stir in the turmeric and the remaining 2 tablespoons of basil.

Serve rice topped with vegetable mixture. Serves 4.

SPANISH RICE

1 cup long-grain brown rice, uncooked
1/4 cup chopped onion
2 small or 1 large clove garlic, minced
1/3 cup chopped green pepper
2 tablespoons water

3 roma chopped tomatoes
1/2 teaspoon chili powder
1/4 teaspoon salt
1/8 teaspoon ground red pepper
1 14 1/2 oz. can beef broth (remove any visible fat)

Coat a non-stick or regular skillet with vegetable spray; place over medium high heat with water. Add rice, onion, garlic, and green pepper; sauté until vegetables are crisp-tender. Stir in tomato and remaining ingredients. Bring to a boil; cover, reduce heat, and simmer 50 minutes, or until rice is tender and liquid is absorbed. Serves 4.

• Brown rice is superior to white rice because it still has the bran. White rice has been milled to remove the germ, and most of the bran.

EAT COLORFULLY

BROWN RICE

1 cup brown rice
2 cups water

The night before or no less than 2 hours before serving, combine rice and water in medium-size saucepan. Let stand.

Bring rice and water to boiling. Lower heat; cover; simmer 20 minutes or until water is absorbed and rice is tender. Serves 2.

BASIC RICE

1 cup brown rice
2 cups water

Bring water to boil. Add rice and reduce heat to simmer. Cover pot and simmer for 45 minutes. Do not lift lid during cooking time. When fully cooked, lift lid fluff grain with a fork. Replace cover, and let rice rest for 5 to 10 minutes. Rice will usually keep in refrigerator for about a week.

- Brown rice contains nine and a half times more minerals than the white. Whole brown rice contains substances that keep the blood vessels elastic much longer.

DESSERTS

APPLE CREPES

2 *large Golden Delicious apples, unpeeled, thinly sliced*
1/4 *cup raisins*
1/4 *cup orange juice*
1/2 *teaspoon corn starch*
1 *teaspoon ground cinnamon*
1 *tablespoon honey*

In medium sauce pan, combine orange juice, corn starch, cinnamon and honey. Stir in apples and raisins. Cook over medium heat, stirring occasionally, 5 to 7 minutes. Make crepes (following page).

To assemble, place 3 tablespoons of mixture on each crepe; roll up around filling. Sprinkle with cinnamon and serve.

May place on non-stick baking sheet in 400 degrees oven for 10 to 12 minutes, for a different texture.
Serves 6.

Variation: Roll up in hot fat-free flour tortillas.

• Apples lower cholesterol and blood pressure, stabilize blood sugar, block some cancers and kill infectious viruses.

CREPES
Easy and fun to make

1 cup whole wheat flour
1 cup evaporated skim milk
1/2 cup water
3 egg whites
1/4 teaspoon salt

Blend flour, milk, egg whites and salt. Heat a small non-stick frying pan. With vegetable spray, lightly spray pan in-between each crepe, if necessary.

Pour 2 tablespoons batter into skillet. Tilt pan quickly to spread batter. Cook over medium heat until top of crepe is dry. Turn over and cook for a few seconds, remove from pan, and cool on clean towel.

Leftover crepes may be frozen between two layers of wax paper. Makes 12 to 15.

CRUSTLESS APPLE PIE

1/4 cup fat-free granola
5 cups sliced cooking apples
1 tablespoon lemon juice
1/4 cup honey
1/4 cup whole wheat flour
1/2 teaspoon cinnamon
1/8 teaspoon nutmeg
1/8 teaspoon cloves
1/8 teaspoon ginger

Preheat oven to 325 degrees.
Grind granola in food processor for 2 minutes; set aside.
Combine all ingredients and pour into a 9 inch oven-proof glass pie dish. Sprinkle top with the ground granola. Bake at 325 degrees for 30 minutes, or until lightly brown and fruit is tender.
Cool on wire rack for 15 minutes. Serves 8.

PIE CRUST

1 1/2 cups fat-free granola
1 tablespoon honey
1 egg white
1 tablespoon frozen apple juice concentrate (thawed)
1 tablespoon cinnamon

Preheat oven to 325 degrees. Process granola in food processor for 2 minutes. Add remaining ingredients and process until just blended (about 20 seconds).

Place in non-stick pie pan and let set for about 10 minutes (will be less sticky).

Press granola mixture over bottom of pan. Bake for 10 to 12 minutes.

- Omit cinnamon if using strawberry filling.

CHERRY STREUSEL

1 can sour pie cherries
1/4 cup honey
2 tablespoons corn starch
1/2 cup cherry liquid
1 teaspoon lemon juice
1/4 teaspoon almond extract
3/4 cup fat-free granola

Drain cherries; reserve liquid. Combine honey and corn starch in saucepan. Gradually add cherry liquid and lemon juice. Blend until smooth. Cook over medium heat, stirring constantly, until thick and clear. Remove from heat. Stir in almond extract and cherries.

Process granola in food processor for 1 minute. In four 8-oz. glass custard cups, place 1 tablespoon of crumbs per cup. Divide cherry filling evenly over granola. Sprinkle remaining granola over tops.

EGG CUSTARD
(Our favorite)

1 12-oz. can evaporated skimmed milk
1 cup soy milk or skim milk
6 large egg whites
1/3 cup honey
1 1/4 teaspoon vanilla

1/2 teaspoon nutmeg

In a large bowl whisk together all ingredients except nut meg. Pour into a 9-inch glass pie plate and sprinkle with nutmeg. Bake in 350 degree oven for 35 to 40 minutes.

This is extra good if you have fresh ripe peaches to layer over the bottom. Serves 4.

PEACH CUSTARD

1 1-lb. can sliced peaches (packed in juice only), drained
1 can evaporated skimmed milk
1 tablespoon oatmeal
1/4 teaspoon nutmeg
1/2 teaspoon cinnamon
1 teaspoon vanilla
4 egg whites
1/4 cup honey

Mix together and stir all ingredients except for peaches. Arrange peaches in pie plate or small baking pan. Pour mixture over peaches and bake in 350 degree oven for 30 minutes. Serves 4.

CRUSTLESS SWEET POTATO PIE

2 *heaping cups firmly packed cooked and diced sweet potato (about 1 large)*
1/2 *cup skim milk or soymilk*
1 *teaspoon vanilla*
1/3 *cup honey*
1 *teaspoon cinnamon*
1/4 *teaspoon ground nutmeg*
1/4 *teaspoon ground clove*
1/4 *teaspoon ground allspice*

Place the potato in container of food processor. Add the remaining ingredients and process until smooth. Pour into pie pan and bake at 350 degrees for 45 to 50 minutes. Serves 6.

CRUSTLESS PUMPKIN PIE

4 egg whites
1/3 cup honey
1 teaspoon cinnamon
1/4 teaspoon salt
1/2 teaspoon ginger
1/4 teaspoon cloves
1/4 teaspoon nutmeg
1 teaspoon almond extract
1 15-oz. can pumpkin
1 1/2 cups evaporated skimmed milk
1 tablespoon whole wheat flour

Preheat oven to 450 degrees. Combine egg whites, honey, flour, almond extract, salt and spices. Blend in pumpkin. Gradually add milk; mix well. Pour into pie plate. Bake at 450 degrees for 10 minutes, then at 350 degrees for 30 minutes, or until a knife inserted about half way between center and outside comes out clean. Serves 6.

FRESH PEACH PIE

5 *cups fresh ripe peaches, peeled and sliced*
1/2 cup frozen apple juice concentrate, thawed
2 tablespoons corn starch
1/4 cup water
1/2 teaspoon cinnamon
1 fat-free pie crust (see page 203)

Prepare pie crust. Cool.

Mash 2 cups of fresh peaches. Add the apple juice concentrate and cinnamon. Whisk corn starch into water and pour into mashed fruit.   Heat to boiling, stirring constantly. Mixture will become a thick, shinny glaze. Fill pie crust with remaining peaches. Pour glaze over top. Chill and serve. Serves 6.

• Can be made with fresh strawberries.

BREAD PUDDING

4 cups whole wheat bread, torn into small pieces
1/4 cup honey
1/4 teaspoon salt
1/2 cup raisins
1 can evaporated skimmed milk
1/2 cup soy milk or skim milk
3 egg whites
1/2 teaspoon cinnamon
1 teaspoon vanilla

Spread bread pieces evenly in 8-inch round glass dish. Drizzle evenly with honey. Sprinkle with raisins and salt. Measure milk into 1 quart measuring cup. Microwave until milk is warm (about 3 to 4 minutes). Add the cinnamon and vanilla and stir. Rapidly stir in egg whites with a fork and mix well. Pour over bread in dish.

Microwave at medium high 9 to 12 minutes, rotating dish half a turn after 6 minutes. Center may still be slightly soft, but will set up as pudding cools. Serve warm or chilled. Serves 4 to 6.

- For baking in oven, place in shallow pan of water. Bake at 350 degrees for 45 minutes.

BANANA CAKE

2 cups whole wheat pastry flour
1 tablespoon baking soda
1/2 teaspoon cream of tartar
1/2 teaspoon cinnamon
1/4 teaspoon nutmeg
1 1/4 cups honey
1 1/2 teaspoon vanilla
4 egg whites
3 very ripe bananas
1/2 cup boiling water
1/2 cup chopped dates

Preheat oven to 325 degrees.

In a large bowl combine flour, baking soda, cream of tartar, cinnamon and nutmeg. Set aside.

In medium bowl, mix honey, vanilla, **2** egg whites, 2 mashed bananas and 1 sliced banana. Stir into flour mixture and mix until just blended.

In blender, puree dates with the water. Stir into flour mixture. Lightly beat the remaining egg whites and gently stir into flour mixture. **Do not overmix.**

Spread into a 9 by 13 inch non-stick baking pan. Bake at 325 degrees for 35 to 40 minutes, or until tooth pick inserted comes out clean.

You may glaze with fruit-juice-sweetened preserves or Banana Topping on following page. Serves 12.

BANANA TOPPING

1/2 cup pure maple syrup
2 small ripe bananas, sliced

In a small saucepan over medium heat, bring syrup to boil. Reduce to medium low and add bananas. Cook for 5 to 7 minutes.

FRUIT TOPPING

2 fresh peaches, sliced
1 cup fresh strawberries, halved
2 teaspoons corn starch
1/4 cup water
1/2 teaspoon cinnamon
1/8 teaspoon allspice

Whisk corn starch into water, heat until thickened. Stir in all remaining ingredients. Cook until boiling.

BLUEBERRY TOPPING

1 *tablespoon corn starch*
1/4 *teaspoon cinnamon*
1/2 *cup water*
2 *tablespoons honey*
2 *cups fresh blueberry*

In small saucepan combine corn starch, cinnamon, water and honey; blend well. Stir in blueberries. Cook over medium heat until mixture boils and thickens, stirring constantly.

•   Good over French toast or pancakes.

STRAWBERRY SAUCE

2 *cups fresh strawberries*
1/4 *cup honey*
2 *tablespoons fresh lemon juice*

Place strawberries, honey and lemon juice in a microwave dish. Cover with plastic wrap, with one end vented and microwave on high for 5 minutes, or until sauce is slightly thick. Serve over fresh fruit (mango, kiwi and pineapple).

BROWN RICE PUDDING

3 cups cooked brown rice (small or medium grain)
3 cups skim milk or soy milk
1/2 cup honey
3 egg whites
1/4 teaspoon salt
2 teaspoons vanilla extract
1/2 teaspoon almond extract
1/2 cup raisins

Combine rice, 2 1/2 cups milk, honey, salt, vanilla and almond extract in medium saucepan. Bring to a boil. Reduce heat. Simmer 20 to 25 minutes, or until very thick and creamy. Stir occasionally. Beat egg whites into remaining milk. Stir into rice mixture. Cook 2 minutes. Refrigerate until chilled. Serves 8 to 10.

BLUEBERRY PUDDING

1 envelope plain unflavored gelatin
1/4 cup boiling water
10 ounces lite tofu, drained
5 tablespoons apple juice concentrate, thawed
1/2 teaspoon vanilla extract
2 tablespoons honey
1/2 teaspoon cinnamon
1 pint fresh blueberries

Dissolve gelatin in boiling water, stirring until crystals disappear.

In a blender, or food processor, blend dissolved gelatin, tofu, apple juice, vanilla, honey, cinnamon and 1 cup of blueberries until smooth. Pour pudding into a bowl; fold in remaining cup of blueberries. Cover with plastic wrap and refrigerate for at least 4 hours. Serves 4.

FRUIT-FILLED MERINGUES

2 egg whites, at room temperature
2 tablespoons maple syrup
1/2 teaspoon lemon juice
1/8 teaspoon cream of tartar

Preheat oven to 275 degrees.

Line a cookie sheet with parchment or brown paper and lightly draw 4 3-inch circles on it with a pencil.

With an electric mixture using a medium bowl, beat the egg whites until bubbly. Add the maple syrup, lemon juice and cream of tartar. Beat on high speed until stiff and glossy, about 3 to 5 minutes. Do not beat until dry.

Spoon or pipe meringue onto paper lined cookie sheet following the outline of each circle, forming a 1-inch rim around sides. Bake on the middle oven rack until justly lightly brown, about 8 to 10 minutes. Turn off oven and leave the meringues in it, with the door closed, for about an hour. Use at once or store in a very tightly covered container for up to a day.

FILLING:

1 cup 1% cottage cheese
1 1/2 tablespoons honey
1 teaspoon vanilla
   Sliced kiwi, strawberries, orange segments

In food processor, or blender, combine cottage cheese, honey and vanilla. Process until smooth. Spoon into meringue shells; top with fruit. Refrigerate. Serves 6.

CHOCOLATE FRUIT BALLS

2 small bananas
1/2 teaspoon coconut extract
1 cup raisins
1 cup chopped dates
1/4 cup WonderSlim cocoa(see page 230)
1 apple, peeled and diced
1 pear peeled and diced
3 tablespoons honey (optional)
2 1/2 cups rolled oats

In a large bowl, mash bananas. Add coconut extract and stir. Mix in remaining ingredients. Refrigerate for a few hours. Process 1/2 cup oats in food processor until a course flour consistency. Shape chocolate fruit into small balls and roll in oats. Cover and refrigerate. We love these frozen.

To mix with food processor:
Place raisins and dates in processor and process for 10 seconds. Add sliced apple and pear. Process a few seconds more - **do not over-process**. Remove and add remaining ingredients.

- Bananas lubricate the intestine and lungs; treats constipation and ulcers. Bananas detoxify the body. They are rich in potassium and are easy to digest.

FRESH FRUIT WITH
FLAX OIL AND YOGURT
Simple and Delicious

1/2 apple or any fresh fruit
1/2 cup plain non-fat yogurt
1 tablespoon flax oil
    Honey to taste
1 teaspoon finely chopped walnuts
    Sprinkle cinnamon and cloves to taste

Combine and mix together until oil is no longer visible.

COTTAGE CHEESE & APPLE
WITH FLAX OIL

1/4 cup 1% cottage cheese
1/2 fresh apple or pear, chopped
1 tablespoon flax oil

Combine and mix together.

Variation: Use unsweetened crushed pineapple on cottage cheese.

BEVERAGES

STRAWBERRY BANANA FREEZIE

1 cup orange juice
2 teaspoons honey
1/2 medium-size ripe banana, sliced
1/2 cup unsweetened strawberries, halved
    Crushed ice

Combine orange juice, honey, banana and strawberries in electric blender. Cover; whirl at high speed until smooth. With motor running, gradually add as much crushed ice as necessary for desired thickness.

WARM APPLE DRINK

3 cups organic apple juice
1/2 teaspoon ground cloves
1/2 teaspoon ground cinnamon
1/2 teaspoon ground allspice
1 tablespoon honey

Combine all ingredients in a saucepan. Heat oven on low heat for 5 minutes. Let stand for 40 to 50 minutes. Reheat to serve.

CHOCOLATE MILK SHAKE

1 cup low-fat soymilk or skim milk
2 teaspoons Wonderslim cocoa (see page 230)
1-2 teaspoons honey
1-2 ice cubes

Put in blender and process for a few minutes or use hand blender.
Variation: Omit cocoa and add 1/2 teaspoon vanilla for vanilla shake.

THICK CHOCOLATE
BANANA SHAKE

1 small banana or 3/4 of a large one
1/2 cup ice water
1/4 cup instant non-fat dry milk powder
     Honey to taste (I use about 1 teaspoon)
1 1/2 teaspoons Wonderslim cocoa (see page 230)
1/2 teaspoon vanilla extract
     Ice cubes

Combine all ingredients except ice cubes in blender or use hand blender. Mix well. Add ice and process until smooth.

* You can buy the dry milk in the bulk bins at the health food store; this allows you to purchase a small amount.

⌨ JOY'S NOTES ⌨

SAUTÉING GARLIC, ONION AND VEGETABLES:

Heat non-stick pan or pan sprayed with vegetable spray over medium heat. Add onion and garlic and 1 to 2 tablespoons of water, broth or wine. Stir often. If onions and garlic stick, add a little more water. Cook until onion and garlic are softened.

POTATOES:

Scrub potatoes, do not peel. The eye and the peeling of the potato contain life-giving properties. When the skin of the potato is not eaten, the best part is lost. Steaming or pressure-cooking them is an excellent way to prepare potatoes. When potatoes are peeled, there is practically nothing left but starch. It has very little food value after it has been peeled and boiled in water that is drained, leaving the potato without minerals. We never peel our potatoes, however, never eat eyes that have grown sprouts. They are toxic.

GARLIC:

Smash it lightly with the bottom of a glass or anything heavy. The peel will slip off easily.

ROASTED GARLIC:

Using a terra cotta garlic roaster, you can roast garlic in the microwave in 1 minute. To roast in oven, wrap in foil and bake until soft, about 30 minutes at 425 degrees.

NUTS:

You may eat a small amount of nuts occasionally. Buy nuts only in the shell. They will last up to one year. Nuts and seeds become rancid and loose their nutrients when they are hulled or shelled. Deterioration begins immediately and continues.

BLACK PEPPER:

Most commercial ground pepper is roasted and is, therefore, an irritant. To make fresh ground pepper, use a pepper mill and whole peppercorn.

EGGS:

Antibiotics are added to chicken feed to keep cooped-up chickens healthy. These feeds replace grains, living insects, and live plant material that they would obtain by roaming free. Free range eggs or yard eggs are a much more nutritious egg, even if we do just eat the whites. Buy large size eggs. Egg shell color is not an indicator of nutritional value. Look for yard eggs at your supper market or health food stores. Also, sometimes your local Farmer's Market will have them. Just ask.

BAKING POWDER:

Most baking powders contain aluminum salt, which accumulates and may cause deterioration of brain cells. Rumford baking powder has no aluminum salt. Your health food stores carry Rumford baking powder.

BREAD:

If you don't have a bread machine, you are really missing a great product. You can make your bread by hand, but it is time consuming. The bread machine is easy and bakes a great loaf of bread.

The other choice would be to check out your bakery department at your health food store. There are a few breads made without hydrogenated oils, but are made with refined flour.

We love our bread machine and make only whole wheat bread.

PITA BREAD:

Buy whole wheat. Kangaroo is a very good brand. You will find it close to your deli at supermarkets.

GARLIC BREAD:

We use Parisien bread and sour dough bread found in the baking department of your local supper market. It is made without oil. However, this is refined flour, so be conservative.

- To prepare: Lightly spray with vegetable spray, sprinkle with garlic powder or you may roast fresh garlic and spread on bread.

FARMER'S MARKET:

Farmer's Markets have locally grown vegetables and fruits and are usually organic.

ALFALFA SPROUTS:

Alfalfa seeds are easy and fun to grow. You can buy seeds at your health food store. Directions come with them. Alfalfa sprouts contain light enzymes.

TOMATOES:

To peel a fresh tomato, cut out the stem end and cut a small x in the rounded end. Plunge the tomato in a pot of rapidly boiling water for 20-60 seconds or until the skin feels loose. Rinse under cold running water and pull the skin off.
To seed a tomato, cut it in half widthwise. Squeeze each half in the palm of your hand, cut side down, to wring out the liquid and seeds.

CORN ON COB:

Cut the ends and tops off to where the corn starts and husk the outer husks off, leaving enough to cover the corn. For 2 ears of corn, microwave on high for 2 minutes, turn over and cook another 2 minutes. The silk and husks come off easily and leave a tastier corn.

BAY LEAVES:

Never eat bay leaves; their sharp edges make them difficult to digest.

BEANS:

Beans are good for you. They are loaded with protein, vitamins, minerals, iron and are high in fiber and complex carbohydrates.

Dried beans cooked from scratch are better for you and better tasting than canned beans.

When you buy loose beans, or break open a package, you need to transfer them to a tightly covered glass or metal container and store in a dry cool place, but not the refrigerator. Save all your empty glass jars to store beans.

Wash and sort beans in a colander.

Beans should always be soaked in water to cover for 4-6 hours prior to cooking. This helps to shorten the cooking time and help eliminate the flatulence problem. Use 3-4 times as much water as beans. Cooked beans can be refrigerated for up to one week.

Refried Beans: Using cooked beans, drain and mash with a hand masher or use a food processor.

Easy Bean Dip: Mix your favorite salsa with refried beans and serve with homemade corn tortilla chips.

- One pound of dry beans yields 6 cups cooked.

Lentils and split peas don't need to be soaked.

Salt should always be added when beans are soft. Otherwise, it toughens the skins. Vinegar and tomatoes have a similar effect.

STEAMING:

An electric steamer is a handy item. You just set it and forget it. A folding steam basket placed in a pan of water does a great job, just not as convenient. However, you can add herbs and seasoning to the water for a nice flavor. You cannot do this with an electric steamer.

Cooking water contains minerals and vitamins and should be saved in preparing other foods, such as, sautéing vegetables.

- Steaming is an excellent method for preserving vitamins. If you microwave, steam, stir-fry or blend in a little water, there will be little decline in your vitamins.

Pressure Cooking: Pressure cooking concentrates nutrients and juices; cooks fast and saves time. We use our pressure cooker a lot. It is especially good for cooking greens.

GINGER ROOT:

You can store fresh ginger root by putting it in a small jar and covering it in vinegar and refrigerate. Will keep up to six months.

FRESH HERBS:

Fresh herbs are the secret to low-fat cooking. Grow your own herbs. It's easy and fun. If you don't have a garden spot, you can grow them in pots. Most herbs are very easy to grow from seeds. However, Rosemary is better purchased as a plant. If you don't want to wait for seeds to grow, you can purchase the little starter plants from your local nursery. The difference between fresh and dried is astounding.

If you buy fresh herbs at the supermarket you can extend their life by wrapping them in a wet paper towel. They can last even longer if you put the ends in a small glass of water and cover with a plastic bag (always refrigerate).

DRIED HERBS AND SPICES:

Remember to add 2 to 3 times more fresh than dried when cooking. Save your small jars (pimento and old spice jars). Fill with dried herbs and spices from the bulk jars at the health food store. Dried herbs and spices have a shelf life of six months. If you grow your own herbs and dry them, the flavor will be far superior to that of store bought. You can grind them in a coffee grinder or food processor.

FRUITS:

Apples are great for you, but they are also one of the most heavily insecticide sprayed fruits. We wash all fruits and vegetables with a fruit wash. Fruit wash is a natural liquid for fruits and vegetables. It removes chemical residue, wax, dirt and bacteria. You can find it in the vitamin section at your health food store.

Another way to remove poison sprays and parasites from produce is soak fruits and vegetables using 1 tablespoon of 3% hydrogen peroxide per 1 gallon of water, or spray with hydrogen peroxide. Wait 1 or 2 minutes, then rinse.

Using Clorox bleach is another method. Add 1/2 teaspoon Clorox to 1 gallon of water. Soak produce for 10 minutes, then in clean water for 10 minutes.

CEREAL:

Check the ingredient list; the first item should be a grain. The shorter the list, the less refined the cereal.

Check the list for grams of fat. Try to choose one that is very low-fat. Look for whole-grain cereal.

• We eat shredded wheat, unsweetned.

SNACKS:

Bake a few sweet potatoes and store in the refrigerator; they taste great cold.

Make popcorn in hot-air corn popper. Lightly spray with vegetable spray and salt to taste.

Dried dates - fresh fruits, plain non-fat yogurt with fresh fruit.

-JOY'S NOTES-

EXTRACTS:

There are artificial versions of extracts found in most supermarkets, but we recommend natural extracts that are alcohol-free. You can find these at your local health food store.

STORAGE:

Store corn meal, rice, flax seed, extra flour, dried herbs and spices in refrigerator. They will stay fresh longer. Keep nuts in freezer.

TORTILLAS:

To make tortilla chips, preheat oven to 400 degrees. Cut corn tortillas into wedges and place on baking sheet that has been lightly sprayed with cooking spray, and bake for 10 to 15 minutes, or until lightly browned. Watch carefully. Once they start to brown, they burn quickly.
For crispy chalupa shells, leave whole.

BUTTERMILK:

Buttermilk is a cultured milk product, like yogurt, that is made by adding special bacterial to non-fat or low-fat milk. A low-fat, nutritional powerhouse, it will keep three weeks in the refrigerator. You can substitute buttermilk for oil or cream in salad dressings. Try it in mashed potatoes - it's great.

Tip: When baking with buttermilk, reduce the amount of baking powder and increase the amount of baking soda instead.

In South Texas, your health food stores carries (Promised Land Dairy) a wonderful brand of buttermilk that has no artificial hormones added. It comes in an old fashioned glass bottle.

WHAT YOU CAN FIND AT YOUR LOCAL HEALTH FOOD STORE (AND MUCH MORE)

Flax seed oil (Barlean's)
Fat-free potato chips (Auburn Farms-sour cream/onions)
Soymilk (WestSoy)
Low-fat and 99.7% caffeine free cocoa (WonderSlim)
Raw-unfiltered apple cider vinegar
Crackers (Health Valley)
Flax seeds (in bulk bin)
Beans and rice (in bulk bin)
Frozen veggie burgers and wieners (Yves)
Dried herbs and spices (bulk)
Vitamins and herbs
Organic products - fat-free pasta sauces, canned beans,
fresh fruits and vegetables
Dried dates (bulk bin)
Stone ground corn meal (bulk bin)
Coffee substitute (Pero, Roma, Cafix and Postum)
Organic juices made not from concentrate
Organic raisins
Organic cereals
Raw honey
Pure maple syrup
Fruit wash
Fat-free Green Giant Harvest Burgers *for recipes*

Go to your local health *food* store when you have some extra time and leisurely browse around each aisle. It's a great place.   We do a lot of shopping at our (Sun Harvest) local health food store.

SUGGESTED FOOD AND ITEMS FOR TRAVELING

Pinto beans
Taquitos
Non-fat cheese sandwiches
Cooked pasta
Purchased pasta sauce
Dates
Fresh fruit
Soups
Green salad
Dry cereal
Bread
Cooked cold sweet potatoes

Electric steamer
Ice Chest
Hot plate
Paper plates/bowls/towels
Utensils
Pans/skillet

We prepare taquitos before we leave on trips. Shop for fresh fruit and vegetables (for the steamer) after a couple of days traveling. Hot plate is used to warm food.

With a little planning and imagination, you can take trips for at least a week without relying on eating at restaurants. We traveled through four states following these guide lines and did great. The money we saved was a plus.

Tip: Purchase dry ice. Wrap in old towels and place in bottom of ice chest. Place crushed or bulk ice on top. This will extend the life of the ice.

KITCHEN ITEMS THAT ARE VERY HELPFUL

Black & Decker steamer
Braun hand blender and chopper
(would be lost without this)
Presto stainless steel pressure cooker
Blender
Food processor
Breadman Bread Machine
Large stainless steel pot
Fat separator
Wooden spoons
Smart chopper (can be found at discount stores)
Good non-stick pan with lid
Terra cotta garlic roaster
Salad spinner
Wire whist
Plastic and glass containers
Hot-air corn popper
Vegetable Slicer

GUIDE FOR SPICES AND HERBS
Enjoy The Spice Of Life

Asparagus:

basil	mustard seed
chives	sage
ginger	savory
lemon balm	tarragon
minced onion	thyme

Beans, dried:

bay leaf	oregano
cilantro	parsley
cumin	sage
garlic	savory
mint	thyme
onions	

Beans, green:

basil	mint
caraway	mustard seed
clove	oregano
curry powder	sage
dill	savory
marjoram	tarragon
minced onion	thyme

Beets:

allspice	ginger
bay leaves	mustard seed
caraway seeds	nutmeg
cloves	tarragon
dill	

Broccoli:

basil	minced onion
dill	nutmeg
garlic	oregano
lemon balm	tarragon
marjoram	thyme

Brussels sprouts:

basil	nutmeg
caraway	savory
dill	tarragon
minced onion	thyme
mustard seed	

Cabbage:

allspice	marjoram
basil	minced onion
caraway	nutmeg
cloves	red pepper
cumin	sage
dill/fennel	savory

Carrots:

allspice	ginger
anise	mace
basil	marjoram
bay leaves	minced onion
chervil	mint
chives	nutmeg
cinnamon	parsley
cloves	sage
cumin	tarragon
dill/fennel	thyme

Cauliflower:

basil	marjoram
caraway seeds	minced onion
chives	paprika
cumin	parsley
dill	rosemary
dry mustard	savory
garlic	tarragon
mace	

Corn:

basil	minced onion
Bay seasoning	nutmeg
chervil	saffron
chives	sage
dry mustard	thyme
lemon balm	

Eggplant:

basil	onion
cinnamon	oregano
dill	parsley
garlic	sage
marjoram	savory
mint	thyme

Fruit:

anise	lemon balm
cinnamon	mint
clove	rosemary
ginger	

Mushrooms:

basil	oregano
coriander	rosemary
curry powder	tarragon
marjoram	thyme

Onions:

caraway	oregano
mustard seeds	sage
nutmeg	thyme

Peas:

allspice	oregano
basil	poppy seeds
caraway	rosemary
chervil	sage
chives	savory
dill/marjoram	tarragon
mint	thyme

Potatoes:

basil	marjoram
caraway	minced onion
chives	oregano
coriander	parsley
dill	rosemary
dry mustard	sage
fennel	tarragon
lovage	thyme

Rice:

basil	saffron
fennel	tarragon
lovage	thyme

Spinach:

anise	marjoram
basil	minced garlic
caraway	minced onion
chervil	nutmeg
chives	oregano
cinnamon	rosemary
dill	savory
mace	thyme

Squash:

basil	minced garlic
caraway	nutmeg
cardamom	oregano
cinnamon	rosemary
clove	sage
dill	savory
ginger	tarragon
marjoram	

Tomatoes:

basil	minced onion
bay leaves	oregano
celery seed	parsley
chives	rosemary
coriander	sage
dill	savory
garlic	tarragon
lovage	thyme
marjoram	

Sweet potatoes:

allspice	cloves
cardamom	ginger
cinnamon	nutmeg

- *To exchange dried for fresh - you double or triple for fresh. If the recipe calls for 2 to 3 tablespoons fresh you can put 1 tablespoon dried.*

- *Crush dried herbs with fingers to rejuvenate them.*

BIBLIOGRAPHY

Balch, James F. M.D. - Balch, Phyllis A. C.N.C. - Prescription For Nutritional Healing - 1990, Avery Publishing Group Inc., Garden City Park, NY

Burnett, George - The Breadman's Healthy Bread Book - 1992, William Morrow and Co., Inc., New York

Cameron, Myra - Lifetime Encyclopedia of Natural Remedies - 1993, Parker Publishing Co., West Nyack, NY

Cawood, Frank W. - The Book of 1,001 Home Health Remedies - 1993, FC&A Publishing, Peachtree City, GA

Charash, Bruce D. M.D. - Heart Myths - 1991, Viking Penguin, NY

Donsbach, Kurt W. D.C., N.D., Ph.D. - Heart Disease, Stroke, Oral & Intravenous Chelation - 1993, The Rockland Corporation, Tulsa

Erasmus, Udo Ph.D. - Fats That Heal, Fats That Kill - 1994, Alive Books, Burnaby BC Canada

The Burton Goldberg Group - Alternative Medicine - 1994, Future Medicine Publishing, Inc., Fife, WA

Heinerman, John Dr. - Healing Power of Herbs - 1995, Globe Communications Corp., Boca Raton, FL

Jones, Paul A. M.D. - The Black Health Library To Heart Disease And Hypertension - 1993, Henry Holt & Co., NY

Kloss, Jethro - Back To Eden - 1994, Back To Eden Publishing Co., Loma Linda, CA

Kogler, Aladar Ph.D. - Yoga For Every Athlete - 1995, Llewellyn Publications, St. Paul, MN

-BIBLIOGRAPHY-

Marx, Ina - Fitness For The Unfit, 1990, Carol Publishing Group, Secaucus, NJ

Mindell, Earl R. Ph., Ph.D. - Earl Mindell's Herb Bible - 1992, Simon & Schuster/Fireside, New York, NY

Mindell, Earl R. Ph., Ph.D. - Earl Mindell's Soy Miracle - 1995, Simon & Schuster/Fireside, New York, NY

Ornish, Dean M.D. - Dr. Dean Ornish's Program For Reversing Heart Disease - 1990, Ballantine Books, NY

Ornish, Dean M.D. - Eat More, Weigh Less - 1993, Harper Collins Publishers, NY

Ornish, Dean M.D. - Stress, Diet And Your Heart - 1984, Penguin Books, New York

Pitchford, Paul - Healing With Whole Foods - 1993, North Atlantic Books, Berkeley, CA

Rawlinson, Ian - Yoga For The West - 1987, CRCS Publications, Sebastopol, CA

Ritchason, Jack N.D., Ph.D., I.D. - The Little Herb Encyclopedia - 1995, Woodland Health Books, Pleasant Grove, UT

Wade, Carlson - Inner Cleansing - 1992, Parker Publishing Co., West Nyack, NY

Vickery, Donald M. M.D. - Fries, James F. M.D. - Take Care Of Yourself - 1992, Addison-Wesley Publishing Co., Inc., NY

Vogel, H.C.A. - The Nature Doctor - 1994, Instant Improvement, Inc., New York, NY

INDEX

INDEX - RECIPES-

To order additional copies of **RECIPE FOR LIFE**, complete the information below.

Ship to: (please print)

Name_____

Address_____

City, State, Zip_____

Day Phone_____

_____ copies of *Recipe For Life* @ $14.95 each $_____

Postage and handling @ $2.50 per book $_____

Texas residents add 7.75% tax ($1.16) per book $_____

Total amount enclosed $_____

Make checks payable to: **Alfie Publishing**

Send to: Alfie Publishing
4817 Eider Drive
Corpus Christi, TX 78413

To order additional copies of **RECIPE FOR LIFE**, complete the information below.

Ship to: (please print)

Name_____

Address_____

City, State, Zip_____

Day Phone_____

_____ copies of *Recipe For Life* @ $14.95 each $_____

Postage and handling @ $2.50 per book $_____

Texas residents add 7.75% tax ($1.16) per book $_____

Total amount enclosed $_____

Make checks payable to: **Alfie Publishing**

Send to: Alfie Publishing
4817 Eider Drive
Corpus Christi, TX 78413

To order additional copies of **RECIPE FOR LIFE**, complete the information below.

Ship to: (please print)

Name_____
Address_____
City, State, Zip_____
Day Phone_____

_____ copies of *Recipe For Life* @ $14.95 each $_____
Postage and handling @ $2.50 per book $_____
Texas residents add 7.75% tax ($1.16) per book $_____
Total amount enclosed $_____

Make checks payable to: **Alfie Publishing**

Send to: Alfie Publishing
4817 Eider Drive
Corpus Christi, TX 78413

To order additional copies of **RECIPE FOR LIFE**, complete the information below.

Ship to: (please print)

Name_____
Address_____
City, State, Zip_____
Day Phone_____

_____ copies of *Recipe For Life* @ $14.95 each $_____
Postage and handling @ $2.50 per book $_____
Texas residents add 7.75% tax ($1.16) per book $_____
Total amount enclosed $_____

Make checks payable to: **Alfie Publishing**

Send to: Alfie Publishing
4817 Eider Drive
Corpus Christi, TX 78413

To order additional copies of **RECIPE FOR LIFE**, complete the information below.

Ship to: (please print)

Name_____

Address_____

City, State, Zip_____

Day Phone_____

_____ copies of *Recipe For Life* @ $14.95 each $_____

Postage and handling @ $2.50 per book $_____

Texas residents add 7.75% tax ($1.16) per book $_____

Total amount enclosed $_____

Make checks payable to: **Alfie Publishing**

Send to: Alfie Publishing
4817 Eider Drive
Corpus Christi, TX 78413

To order additional copies of **RECIPE FOR LIFE**, complete the information below.

Ship to: (please print)

Name_____

Address_____

City, State, Zip_____

Day Phone_____

_____ copies of *Recipe For Life* @ $14.95 each $_____

Postage and handling @ $2.50 per book $_____

Texas residents add 7.75% tax ($1.16) per book $_____

Total amount enclosed $_____

Make checks payable to: **Alfie Publishing**

Send to: Alfie Publishing
4817 Eider Drive
Corpus Christi, TX 78413